The Great Glen Way

The Great Glen Way

A Low-Level Walking Route from Fort William to Inverness

**Heather Connon
and Paul Roper**

MAINSTREAM
PUBLISHING

EDINBURGH AND LONDON

First published in Great Britain in 1997 by
MAINSTREAM PUBLISHING COMPANY (EDINBURGH) LTD
7 Albany Street
Edinburgh EH1 3UG

ISBN 1 85158 864 7

A catalogue record for this book is available from the British Library

Typeset in Garamond
Printed in Great Britain by The Cromwell Press, Melksham

To Asyet

Contents

Introduction

The Great Glen Way is a 71-mile (114km) walk across Scotland from the Atlantic Ocean in the west to the North Sea in the east. On its way, it passes the foot of Ben Nevis, Britain's highest mountain; goes round the shore of Loch Ness, its largest loch (complete with friendly monster); along the banks of the Caledonian Canal, still one of the greatest engineering feats ever achieved in Britain; and past castles and forts which have witnessed some of the most bloody scenes of Scotland's history.

All this is against a backdrop of some of the most spectacular scenery Scotland has to offer. There is the tranquil beauty of Loch Oich; the towering majesty of the Nevis range; the turbulent history of Achnacarry and the Dark Mile; the charm of the whitewashed canal buildings at Kytra Lock; and the barren beauty of the moorland above the Glen. It is a land teeming with wildlife, from deer and wildcat through osprey and buzzard to heather and saxifrage; all will combine to enchant you as you walk the Way.

The star of the walk is the Great Glen itself. Described by W.H. Murray, climber and author of classic travel guides, as a 'geological freak of the highest order', it was formed 380 million years ago when the north of Scotland shifted 65 miles to the south-west relative to the rest, along a huge fault-line which runs the width of the country. The hills and lochs which characterise the

Glen today were carved out far more recently, a mere 20,000 years ago, when the huge glaciers which scoured Scotland during the Ice Age found that the weak line of the fault offered least resistance. The result is a yawning chasm, bordered by towering hills and floored with deep lochs, like a giant corridor through the country.

The small strips of land between the Glen's three lochs (Loch Lochy, Loch Oich and Loch Ness) keep the two parts of Scotland together, but it was a close thing: had the glaciers dug another 50m deep, the whole of the north of Scotland would have been an island. The hills, lochs and Glen may now look finished and fully formed, but the fault which created them is still the most active in Britain. The Great Glen area has more earthquakes than anywhere else in the country – 60 in the last two centuries – the strongest being in August 1816, when walls and chimneys in Inverness cracked under the force of the vibrations.

The Great Glen Way is also an introduction to Scotland's turbulent history. Walking it takes you on a tour of the country's past, from the Iron Age, when the Great Glen gave access to the north-east of Scotland to tribes from Ireland, through the power struggles and bloody battles of the medieval period to the daring exploits of Bonnie Prince Charlie, who made the Great Glen his own as he fought to win back the Scottish crown for his father.

The Glen owes its pivotal place in Scotland's history to its unique geography. With no hills between the east and west coasts, it offers one of the easiest routes from one side of the country to the other, while travellers from the north of Scotland have no option but to cross it on their journey south. Anyone controlling the Glen could, therefore, effectively control the movement of much of

The early stages of the Great Glen Way follow the towpaths of the Caledonian Canal

the Highland population – a much sought-after prize, as the number of forts and castles along its length demonstrates.

The Glen's geography and strategic importance made it an obvious route for developing communications. First came General Wade who built a network of roads as part of the Government's attempt to subdue the unruly Highlanders. Then there came railway lines and, finally, the Caledonian Canal. The Great Glen Way makes full use of all these lines of communication on its journey across Scotland, walking on Wade's roads, the abandoned railway tracks and the canal towpath. This makes the Great Glen Way an excellent long-distance path with easy walking and straightforward route-finding. Although you will have to consult maps and study the instructions in this book, the route is not difficult to follow, leaving plenty of time to savour the countryside and imagine its turbulent history.

The Way is suitable for walkers of all levels of ability. There is little climbing on the route itself, but there are plenty of opportunities for more experienced walkers to venture into the hills and glens which surround it. The walk can be done quickly or slowly, and with as much comfort as you wish. Accommodation along the route is varied, ranging from basic hostels and campsites to luxury hotels.

The Great Glen may be one of Scotland's most famous features, but the Great Glen Way is a hidden gem. The canal towpath is little used and delightfully peaceful. The rest of the route takes quiet forest paths, deserted sections of the abandoned railway and minor roads through stretches of open moorland. To walk the Great Glen Way is to enjoy the peace of the countryside. But the route is also very accessible. There is a train station at either end of the route and a regular bus service along its length, making it easy to break the walk up into shorter sections, if required.

There is much in the countryside to enjoy. There are the man-made attractions, such as castles and forts, all with tales to tell of Scotland's turbulent past; the military roads, canal bridges and railways, a constant reminder of the advance of communications through the Great Glen. Then there is the natural beauty of the Glen itself: the towering hills which accentuate its long, straight path across the country; the delightful forests with their mixture of ancient woodland and recently planted conifers; the bright colours of the plants and shrubs which line its floor; and the birds and animals which inhabit its braes and glens.

This book provides all the information you need to enjoy the walk to the full. There are detailed instructions on how to follow each section of the route, descriptions of the history and geography of the Glen, and information on the plants and wildlife you will encounter as you walk.

The Great Glen Way is an enjoyable walk across Scotland. To get the most out of it, you should be prepared and properly equipped. The next chapter contains useful information on long-distance walking to help your preparation.

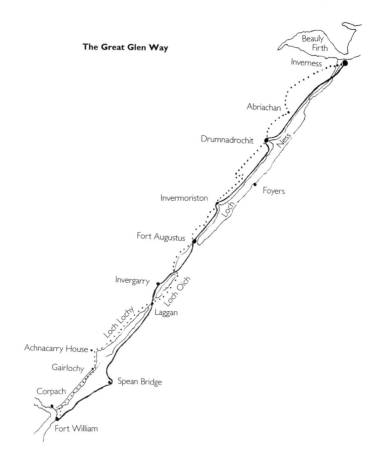

The Great Glen Way

Beauly
Firth

Inverness

Abriachan

Drumnadrochit

Ness

Foyers

Invermoriston

Loch

Fort Augustus

Invergarry

Loch Oich

Loch Lochy

Laggan

Achnacarry House

Gairlochy

Spean Bridge

Corpach

Fort William

14

Walking the Great Glen Way

The Great Glen Way is a long-distance footpath from Fort William to Inverness. The walking is straight-forward – apart from two short stretches, it is on towpaths, forest tracks and minor roads, with only short sections of climbing – but it should still be taken seriously. It is a long walk: 71 miles (114km) and will take up to seven days to complete – or longer if you decide to tackle the excursions suggested along the way. To enjoy it to the full, you should be well prepared, suitably equipped (but not overloaded with gear) and confident of your ability to follow directions on a map.

The route is not waymarked, so you will have to consult this book and your maps regularly. It is important that you plan each day's walking carefully; although it may look as if the route is obvious, it is easy to miss a turning or be fooled into taking the wrong path – particularly in forests, where there may be tracks and smaller paths deviating from the main route. Scottish Natural Heritage have proposed a long-distance path through the Great Glen, which is likely to follow the route described in this book. At the time of writing, it was still awaiting government approval and it will take at least two years after that is received until the waymarkers and other pieces of route information are in place.

The Great Glen Way is a rewarding walk which will take you through some of the wildest and most romantic countryside Scotland has to offer. This section gives advice on how to prepare yourself to get the most out of the walk. Much of it is common sense and will be familiar to anyone with experience in long-distance walking. It is worth repeating, however: the better prepared you are, the more you will enjoy the walk.

PLANNING THE ROUTE

Although the Great Glen Way is almost entirely on established paths and tracks, it does pass through some isolated areas, where the nearest house – never mind shop or hotel – can be some distance away. Accommodation outside the main centres like Fort Augustus and Drumnadrochit is scarce and, even in these towns, can be fully booked well in advance in the height of the summer. If you are relying on staying in bed and breakfasts or hotels, you should plan each day's walk carefully to ensure you will find somewhere to stay at night. Those relying on camping and youth hostels will have to be equally prepared. There are campsites and areas for wild camping along the Glen, but these too can be busy in high season. You will find official youth hostels in Fort William, Laggan, on the shores of Loch Ness beyond Invermoriston and in Inverness, and other hostel and bunkhouse-type accommodation in Fort Augustus and Drumnadrochit. Again, these can be very busy.

All walkers go at their own pace; only you will know how far you can realistically travel in a day. As you will see when you look at the route, it is easy to break it down into daily sections which will get you from Fort William to Inverness in five to seven days, covering between ten and 16 miles (16 and 25km) a day. You should plan your pace to suit the slowest member of the group. Naismith's rule is a useful guide to plan how far you will travel in a day. It suggests that the average walking speed is three miles an hour, less if the route is climbing steeply. Remember this is only an average; carrying a heavy load, hot or cold weather, rain and wind will all affect your pace. You should also allow yourself plenty of time to enjoy the route: the scenery is spectacular and there are many places where you will want to linger to admire the view or take a short detour to places of interest just off the route.

Accommodation details change frequently, and many places are only open at certain times of the year. This book does not, therefore, provide a list of places to stay. These can be obtained from the local tourist information offices which you should contact for details of accommodation before setting out. To be sure of getting a bed each night, you should book ahead, particularly in high season when you will be competing with other tourists visiting the Great Glen by car, bus and boat. Do telephone ahead if your plans change and you decide to stay elsewhere – it could save a lot of worry and the expense of alerting the rescue services.

FOLLOWING THE ROUTE

As already mentioned, the Great Glen Way is not waymarked. In some sections it takes the same route as the Great Glen Cycle Route, but in other parts the cyclists follow a completely different path, so you cannot rely on their signposts to keep you heading in the right direction. The distinctive geography of the Great Glen makes the general direction obvious: you are following

Looking along Loch Ness

the long valley from one end to the other. Sometimes you will be walking along the floor of the Glen, while at other times you will be on the hills which tower above it. Often, there will be a number of different ways to get from place to place in the Glen; the Great Glen Way chooses the most scenic, the safest and the quietest of these. It is therefore important that you study the route carefully before setting out on each section. You will not

want to have to refer constantly to a book as you walk along, so it is suggested that you draw the route on your map after studying the directions in this book.

Do not attempt the route without a map and knowledge of how to read it. Although there is only one brief section where the Great Glen Way goes across open countryside, a map is useful along the entire length of the route. It will make sure you stay on the correct path, and

19

help you get back to it quickly should you stray from it. It will also help you to pinpoint interesting features along the Way, whether they be villages, Iron Age forts or battle sites. The three maps suggested for the Great Glen Way are in the Ordnance Survey Landranger series:

Sheet 41 Ben Nevis and Fort William
Sheet 34 Fort Augustus and Glen Albyn
Sheet 26 Inverness and Strathglass.

Those who plan to wander off the route on the diversions and excursions suggested in the book or to climb some of the other hills which border the Great Glen should also have a compass and appropriate hillwalking equipment like extra warm clothes and emergency food supplies. The hills may look inviting from the safety of the Great Glen, but climb into them and you will find yourself in wild, remote areas where the nearest telephone to summon help can be some miles away. It is easy to get disoriented on the hills on the clearest day; in poor visibility, even the most experienced walkers will need careful compass work to be sure of staying on the right track. You should not venture into the hills unless you are certain that everyone in the party has the skills to cope with the terrain.

Every effort has been made to ensure the information in this book is comprehensive and accurate. No responsibility can be taken for any errors or omissions but the authors would be glad to hear if you come across any so that subsequent editions can be updated.

WHEN TO GO

You can do the Great Glen Way any time of the year and every season has its attractions. In spring, when the trees are in bud and the wildflowers are beginning to bloom, the countryside looks fresh and new. The later spring months are often blessed with dry, mild days and clear air which give expansive views across the surrounding hills. It will also be quieter than the summer months and accommodation will be easier to find (although some places will remain closed until well after Easter). In summer, the days are long and the climate is at its best, although conditions are often rather wetter than in late spring. The trees will be bearing flowers and fruit and the plants and flowers in the verges are at their most profuse. In autumn, the colours of Scotland are at their finest: the reds and russet of the leaves glow against a backdrop of hills ablaze with purple heather and golden bracken. The summer crowds will have died down once again and the paths are likely to be quieter and accommodation less in demand. Winter can be the best time in Scotland. The hills are at their most majestic when they are snow-covered and their peaks framed against a clear blue sky. The highest point on the Great Glen Way is just over 350m, and much of the walking is close to sea level, so the route should be easily passable without specialist walking equipment for most of the year. Fierce blizzards can block the roads, however, making access to the Way difficult. Many hotels and guest-houses close in winter as well, so you will have to plan the route carefully and book accommodation in advance.

The book describes the route going from west to east although you can, of course, walk it in the opposite direction. The small sections of climbing lie between Fort Augustus and Inverness, so those who start in the west will have had plenty of time to get their legs and feet used to walking before testing them further with a few steep slopes. By starting at Fort William and ending in

Inverness, the prevailing wind is kept behind, rather than in front – and you will certainly feel the difference if the wind changes direction to come from the east. The climate gets steadily drier, if a little cooler, along the Glen. Fort William is one of the mildest and wettest areas of Britain, with an average annual rainfall of 2m (80 inches). Rainfall drops almost an inch for every mile you walk east from Fort William so that, by Inverness, the average has dropped to just 65cm (25 inches) a year.

That said, there can be rain – not to mention snow, hail, strong winds and brilliant sunshine – on any day in Scotland. Whichever time of year you choose to walk the route, be prepared for all weathers.

CLOTHING AND EQUIPMENT

The first rule of long-distance walking is to take as little as possible – remember, everything you pack you carry. The weight of the pack will depend on whether you are relying on bed and breakfasts and hotels (in which case a change of clothes is all that is necessary) or camping, when a tent, sleeping-bag and cooking equipment will also be required.

Whatever accommodation is chosen, it is essential to balance the need to have a light pack with the requirement to keep safe and warm on the walk. The weather can change quickly and, even in summer, a warm layer such as a fleece or sweatshirt as well as a waterproof jacket and trousers should be carried. Gaiters are useful for keeping feet dry when the weather is wet. Gloves and a hat will be very welcome in wintry conditions. A survival bag is also useful; although the route does not go into wild, open countryside, it does pass through remote areas where you can be some way from help. If any member of the party does become ill or get injured, a survival bag will help keep them warm until help arrives. Thick plastic survival bags can be bought cheaply at any outdoor shop. A whistle, torch, compass, first-aid kit and emergency food rations are also a necessary part of any walking kit.

The most important piece of equipment is not in your pack but on your feet. Strong, comfortable walking boots are essential for tackling the Great Glen Way: trainers and sandals may be fine for day walks along canal paths, but they are much less comfortable for walking continuously for five days or more, carrying a pack. Boots should be waterproof and sturdy enough to support the ankles on some of the rougher terrain on the route. They should also be well worn-in; nothing is more certain to cause blisters than starting a long walk wearing new boots. Even old boots can occasionally cause blisters and sore feet. Attend to these immediately; the longer they are left, the worse they will get. Blisters and other aches and pains are less likely to be a problem if you are fit for walking. A few weekends' practice with a full pack and boots will make the first days of the route, when you are getting used to carrying your rucksack and the rhythm of walking, all the more enjoyable.

Although the Great Glen is a popular tourist area, even basic services like shops can be some way apart, particularly on the quiet routes followed by the Way. There is, for example, no bank or shop between Fort William and Fort Augustus, although one shop can be found a short way off the route at Laggan Bridge. From then on, services are a little more plentiful, although there is no shop, pub or tearoom for the entire 26km (16 miles) from Drumnadrochit to Inverness. It is essential to plan ahead to make sure you have sufficient funds and food stocks for the route.

THE COUNTRY CODE

For most of its length, the Great Glen Way follows public paths, forest tracks and roads on which there is a recognised right of way, so access on the route should not be a problem. Please note that the inclusion of a route in the book does not imply that it is a right of way. All the land surrounding the route – and most of the paths and tracks – belong to someone, whether it be the British Waterways Board, Forest Enterprise or a private landowner. Respect their rights by treating their land with courtesy and consideration; doing so will ensure that the owners remain well disposed to walkers. This means following the countryside code:

1. Guard against the risk of fire.
2. Fasten all gates. Use gates and stiles where possible. If it is necessary to climb a fence or wall, take care not to damage it.
3. Keep dogs under control.
4. Keep to paths where they exist. Circling round boggy sections or taking shortcuts on zigzags extends the area of erosion.
5. Leave no litter.
6. Safeguard water supplies. Do not pollute burns and streams; toilet well away from them.
7. Protect wildlife, plants and trees.
8. Go carefully on country roads.
9. Respect the life and work of the countryside.

Parts of the Great Glen are prime sheep-farming country. Take particular care when walking the Way in the lambing season in April and May, when some detours may be needed to avoid disturbing the animals. There will also be some grouse-shooting and deer-stalking between July and December, although (apart from the suggested excursion up Sron a' Choire Ghairbh) the route does not stray into affected areas.

Many of the forests on the route are commercial plantations, where the timber is regularly harvested for sale. You should watch out for signs that tree-felling is in progress and avoid these areas where possible. If you have no option but to pass the working area, take great care. Ensure that the operators of any logging machinery are aware of your presence, and wait until they signal it is safe before proceeding. Leave the area as quickly as possible. Do not be tempted to use as picnic seats the piles of timber which lie beside some of the paths; they are easily dislodged, and once the logs start rolling, they are impossible to stop.

The Great Glen Way is a challenging walk. It will also be an enjoyable holiday for those who embark upon it well prepared and fully equipped. A few hours spent planning the route will be time well spent, repaying itself many times over in satisfaction from a walk well done.

Tourist Information Offices
Fort William: 01397 703781
Fort Augustus: 01320 366367
Inverness: 01463 234353

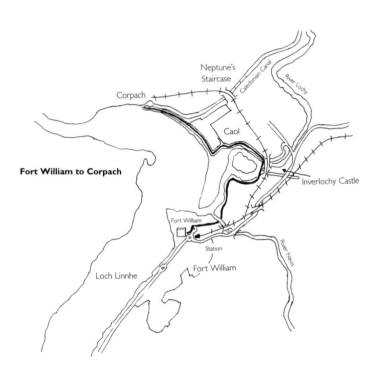

Fort William to Corpach

Neptune's
Staircase

Corpach

Caledonian Canal

River Lochy

Caol

Inverlochy Castle

Fort William

Station

River Nevis

Loch Linnhe

Fort William

Section 1
Fort William to Corpach

The Great Glen Way starts at Fort William, a bustling town strung out along the banks of Loch Linnhe. It is the undisputed capital of the West Highlands, a natural stopping place for those heading north from Glen Coe, south from Skye and the Western Isles or west from Aviemore and Glen Spean – as will be clear from the crowds of walkers, climbers, sailors, tourists, and even a smattering of locals, who daily crowd its long main street.

In the mid-19th century, it was described as 'the heart of a district abounding with wild, romantic scenery', and it is certainly preferable to concentrate on the surrounding countryside rather than the town itself. Apart from the plentiful shops, banks and other amenities which will allow you to stock up on last-minute essentials, Fort William has little to recommend it. Frank Fraser Darling, the Scottish naturalist, called it 'an eyesore'; M.E.M. Donaldson, whose travel writings published early in the 20th century are classics of their time, was even ruder, describing the town as 'one of the few places in the Highlands to which you only go so that you may get away from it and on to somewhere else with all possible speed'.

Walking the Great Glen Way is hardly escaping with 'all possible speed', but it does soon get you out into some glorious countryside. For, whatever you may think of Fort William, there can be no disputing that its position as a gateway to the scenery and challenges of the great outdoors is unparalleled. It stands in the shadow of Ben Nevis – although, from much of the town, the mighty 1,344m (4,406ft) summit of Britain's highest mountain is concealed behind Cow Hill, a pimple in comparison at just 287m.

Perhaps the best place to appreciate Fort William's magnificent surroundings is to climb Cow Hill, a pleasant evening stroll should you arrive in the town early. From there, you get a grandstand view of the brooding massif of Ben Nevis and the Mamores as well as north and west across Loch Linnhe and Loch Eil to the splendid hills of Ardgour. Those who arrived in Fort William by road will already have been entranced by the beauty of Loch Linnhe, one of the finest lochs to drive along. The view from the top of Cow Hill will confirm it as one of the most dazzling stretches of water that Scotland has to offer.

More interesting to Great Glen Way walkers is the view to the north, where it is already possible to identify the shape of the Glen and to pick out the paths of the River Lochy and the Caledonian Canal as they wind their way in tandem towards Loch Lochy. Some of the landmarks of the early sections of the walk are already clear, like the pepperpot lighthouse at Corpach, which marks the start of the canal, and Neptune's Staircase, the ladder of locks about 1.5km (one mile) along it.

If nothing else, Fort William deserves its poor reputation as a tourist centre for its cavalier attitude to its venerable history. It has within its perimeter two of the most famous buildings in Scottish history: the garrison, to which it owes its name, and Inverlochy Castle. Yet the first has all but disappeared, swallowed up to make way for the railway station, and the latter is fenced off and in ruins, although there are encouraging signs that repairs are now being considered to make the castle safe. Similarly, the Great Glen Way passes across the site of one of Scotland's most memorable battles – the Battle of Inverlochy – yet there is not even a commemorative plaque to mark the event.

The garrison, or fort, marks the official start of the Great Glen Way but, given the lack of evidence of its existence, you would do better to follow the signs for the railway station or An Aird than to look for battlements and fortified walls. There are a few remnants of the fort on the banks of Loch Lochy just opposite the railway station and the supermarket carpark. The supermarket, which has a brief history of the town in the entrance foyer, is a good place to stock up on last-minute requirements for the walk.

Although the town is now named after its fort, the garrison was not originally called Fort William. General Monck, who built the fort, christened it Inverlochy in a letter to Oliver Cromwell on 22 June 1654 telling him of its completion. It was to the next King of England, the Dutchman William of Orange, that the fort and the town now owe their name.

The Fort William garrison was one of three built in the Great Glen on the orders of Oliver Cromwell. The Great Glen Way also passes the other two: at Fort Augustus halfway along the route and at its end point in Inverness. Here, Monck's main aim was to subdue the troublesome Clan Cameron, a purpose which he singularly failed to achieve. Indeed, the Cameron chiefs seem to have spent most of their time cheekily snubbing their noses at the government forces trying to keep order in the area, starting almost as soon as the fort was built.

Unlike its counterpart in Fort Augustus, this fort did manage to withstand two attacks on it. The first was led by General Gordon during the 1715 rebellion, and the second by Sir Ewen Cameron in 1746. The defending officers in the later siege were rewarded with a visit from the Duke of Cumberland, fresh from his victory at Culloden, who visited the fort in 1746 and permitted the officers to kiss his ring in recognition of their sterling efforts!

What finally put paid to the fort was not fighting but the march of progress. Troops were withdrawn from it following the outbreak of the Crimean War around 1853 and it was dismantled in 1864. Twenty-five years later it was sold to the West Highland Railway company, and the station and tracks built on the site.

From the remains of the fort on the lochside, cross the road and head along the footpath which runs to the right of the McDonald's restaurant. If you are starting off on a Saturday you may be treated to a display of shinty, the famous Highland game similar to hockey, being played by local teams on the ground to the right of the path.

The Way continues across the River Nevis on a road bridge, now closed to traffic. Wade's Road, which lies at the other side of the bridge, marks the start of his route through the Great Glen to Inverness, constructed between the 1715 and 1745 rebellions as part of the government's strategy to subdue the unruly Highlanders. You do not follow Wade's Road, but instead turn immediately left down a rough track which leads to the banks of the River Lochy. The river will remain a feature of the Way for the rest of this section and the next until it reaches its source at Gairlochy. Take care on the boggier sections and the makeshift bridges which can be rather slippery. There are plans to improve this area which, hopefully, will include resurfacing the path and making the bridges more substantial.

The area around the path may look like a patch of scruffy meadowland but, if you close your eyes and concentrate hard, you may be able to conjure up the screams of battle. This is the site of the Battle of Inverlochy, one of the greatest in Highland history and the finest hour of the Marquis of Montrose, Scotland's most neglected hero. It took place on 2 February 1645 and combined all the essential elements of great battles: daring and ingenuity by a great leader; an arrogant and deeply unpopular enemy; and a convincing victory for the underdog.

The royalist Montrose was returning to Aberdeen through the Great Glen, having just ravaged the county of Argyll. With about 1,800 men drawn from the Donald, Cameron and Stewart clans, he was camped by Kilcumein (now Fort Augustus). As he was contemplating an advance to Inverness, the Gaelic poet Iain Lom MacDonald warned him that the Duke of Argyll's army, made up largely of Campbells, was on his tail and was camped with 3,000 men at Inverlochy.

Montrose realised he had to react to the threat, or risk being trapped between Argyll's men heading north-east from Fort William and forces coming down the Glen from Inverness. The obvious solution was to face the threat head-on by marching down the Glen, but that would have given Argyll's men plenty of time to prepare for a set-piece battle. Instead, Montrose and his men, aptly dubbed 'Scotland's army of mountaineers' by the climber and travel writer W.H. Murray, decided to take a 'devious and hitherto untrodden' way, across the Corrieyairack Pass and around the foothills of the Grey Corries and Ben Nevis. The 48km (30-mile) journey took two days and two nights, climbed as high as 752m (2,500ft) at the summit of the Corrieyairack and was carried out in driving snow and freezing temperatures, the men surviving their ordeal on drammoch, a mixture of oatmeal and water. It succeeded admirably in surprising the enemy.

Argyll could not believe that all Montrose's men could have made it down Glen Nevis, and his own soldiers were taken by surprise. Montrose's army had already perfected the rather unorthodox fighting style known as the Highland Charge, which won the Scots victory in so many battles (but which was to prove their undoing at Culloden). It involved a screaming charge by the clansmen until they were close enough to wreak devastation with claymore and dirk. M.E.M. Donaldson, in his book *Wanderings in the Western Highlands and Islands*, describes it well. The Highlanders' strategy was to wait until they could fire 'into the beards' of the enemy. Ranked shoulder to shoulder, they charged in an impetuous rush, holding their fire until they were almost face to face with Argyll's men. Then, they bent on their left knee so that their swords or bayonets could be sure of hitting the target.

This unusual fighting method, combined with the surprise of the attack, meant that Montrose's royalists quickly overcame Argyll's men. More than half the enemy were killed, despite their great superiority in numbers, while Montrose's army suffered just four casualties and a further hundred men wounded.

The victory was immortalised in verse by Iain Lom in *The Day of Inverlochy*, part of which goes as follows:

Warm your welcome was at Lochy
With blows and buffets thickening round you
And Clan Donald's grooved claymore
Flashing terror to confound you

On the wings of eagle rumour
Far and wide the tale is flying
How the slippery knaves the Campbells
With their cloven skills are lying . . .
Fallen race of Diarmid, disloyal, untrue
No harp in the Highlands will sorrow for you.

If Montrose was the hero then Argyll surely qualified as coward of the battle. Instead of fighting alongside his troops, as Donaldson puts it, he 'made haste to secure the possession most precious to him in the world – his own personal safety'. He fled to a galley on Loch Linnhe where he was rescued and sailed safely away.

It was Montrose's sixth victory against the Covenanters but his success was not to last long. Five years later, he was betrayed by MacLeod of Assynt and hanged in Edinburgh; Campbell of Argyll, a coward to the last, watched the execution from behind a curtain.

Fort William is not just the tourist capital of the western Highlands, it is also the industrial capital and, from here, there is plenty of evidence of that. Ahead on the left, just at the top of Loch Linnhe, is the massive grey bulk of the Corpach pulp mill, established in 1966 and now owned by the Arjo Wiggins international paper company.

While converting trees into paper may be an obvious activity for an area so rich in forestry, Fort William's other major industry is rather less expected: aluminium smelting. The chimney stacks off to the right of the path mark the British Alcan aluminium smelter which lies beneath the slopes of Meall an t-Suidhe. Like the pulp mill, it was the abundant natural resources which brought the smelter here; in this case, water. Millions of gallons are pumped along a 24km (15-mile) pipeline through the heart of Ben Nevis from Loch Laggan and Loch Treig to drive the Inverlochy power station which supplies the smelter's power.

The force of that water will be all too clear as you cross the bridge over the tailrace from the power station. When the water is in full flow, the roar as it passes under the bridge is deafening. It is fierce enough to set the bridge humming – and your head spinning as you gaze down at the racing waters.

At the other end of the battlefield are the ruins of Inverlochy Castle. There is evidence of fortification here stretching as far back as AD273, when Donald of the Isles is said to have been murdered in a building called Inverlochy Castle; and in the ninth century the emperor Charlemagne is reputed to have met the Pictish king Achaius on a site near here. The current building probably dates from around 1260, however, when it was built by Sir John Comyn, known as the Black Lord of Badenoch, whose ancestors came to Britain with William the Conqueror.

Once, its walls stood 9m (30ft) tall and 3m (9ft) thick, enclosing a courtyard measuring 27m (90ft) by 30m (100ft). There are also traces of a moat which circled the castle about 12m (40ft) from its walls. Some evidence of its eventful past was unearthed during a brief (and quickly abandoned) attempt at renovation in the late 19th century. A complete male skeleton was discovered, walled up in the northern extremity of the parapet passage.

For the best views of the castle, albeit still obscured by fencing and scaffolding, go under the railway tunnel just before the long wooden bridge which takes you over the River Lochy.

From the tailrace, climb the steps up to the footbridge

Inverlochy Castle

35

which crosses the River Lochy alongside the railway. Still known locally as 'the soldiers' bridge', it was built by the Royal Engineers as part of a civilian defence exercise. The railway track carries trains on the West Highland Line from Fort William to Mallaig, which is deservedly rated as one of the most beautiful railway journeys of the world.

Coming down from the bridge, you arrive on the Caol peninsula. A narrow strip of land bordered on one side by the River Lochy and on the other by the Caledonian Canal, it stretches all the way from here to Gairlochy. The Great Glen Way follows it for all of that distance. As you step down on to it from the bridge, cross the road – watching out for traffic which hurtles over the blind summit on the right – turn left and continue down the road past the school and round the bend towards Caol. The road winds around to the right, at which point you should cross it and head left down Glenmallie Road which leads to the foreshore of Loch Linnhe. There are fine views back to Fort William and to the hills which surround the loch. The wind whips up between these hills from the Atlantic Ocean and, if it is a cold day, you will be glad that the more sheltered areas of the Great Glen lie ahead. Once you are in the Glen, unless you are unlucky, the wind should lie behind you all the way to Inverness.

Shortly before Corpach, a small shopping centre gives a last chance to stock up on food, stamps and other requirements. After Corpach, there are no more shops until the Way reaches Fort Augustus, 50km (30 miles) ahead. The path stays on the foreshore until it reaches Corpach basin and the start of the Caledonian Canal. As it reaches the canal, the Great Glen Way turns north-east and continues along the towpath into the Great Glen. But, having come so close to the start of the Caledonian Canal, it is worth a detour to inspect it up close.

Instead of going right immediately, turn left and head down to the sea loch and the pepperpot lighthouse which marks the start of the canal. If you take the detour to Clachnacharry at the end of the Way, you will be able to boast that you have walked across Scotland from sea to sea.

The pepperpot is the most distinctive building at Corpach. It is one of five on the canal – the others are at the entrance to Loch Lochy at Gairlochy, marking the entrance to the canal in Fort Augustus from Loch Ness, at the confluence of Lochs Ness and Dochfour, and at the canal's end in Inverness. All were once

The beginning of the Caledonian Canal at Corpach

37

occupied and operated manually but are now automatic.

One of the first buildings on the canal was constructed here: a brewery. It was hoped that the navvies employed to build the canal could be weaned off their fondness for whisky by drinking beer instead. The ploy was, by all accounts, a failure; the navvies simply took the opportunity to have a pint of beer to accompany their drams.

Corpach boasted a shipbuilder for a brief spell after the canal was completed, but trade was insufficient and it closed. Long before that, it was home to a smithy, famous for its broadswords. These were much in demand by local clan chiefs and are mentioned by Sir Walter Scott in his novel *Tales of a Grandfather*.

Corpach means 'City of the Dead', and is so called because Scottish kings were taken from here across the sea to Iona for burial. More prosaically, William T. Kilgour, who found fame with his writings on life on Ben Nevis when the observatory was there, notes that it was necessary to keep the bodies on this island to prevent them being eaten by wild animals or stolen by bodysnatchers. Nowadays, the village has a number of houses offering bed and breakfast, a couple of pubs and shops and a fascinating museum, Treasures of the Earth, which houses a collection of gemstones and minerals. To get to Corpach, turn left just beyond the basin and cross the railway line. To continue on the Way, cross the canal again and turn left to carry on along the towpath.

Pause a moment or two before continuing along the Way to savour the views back towards Fort William. This is a favourite spot for taking photographs of Ben Nevis, as its entire lowering bulk can be seen to great advantage from this aspect. Many more excellent perspectives lie ahead of you, however. Having savoured this view, you are ready to set off into the Great Glen for the journey towards Inverness.

The Caledonian Canal

The further you walk through the Great Glen, the easier it is to understand why the Caledonian Canal seemed such a good idea. Its very geography makes the route obvious; not only did the geological fault create a natural passage from one end of Scotland to the other, but the three lochs which were gouged out by the glaciers which scoured the Glen meant that much of it was ready-made; of the canal's 60 miles (96km), only 22 (35km) had to be man-made; for the other 38 (68km), boats use the natural waterways of Loch Lochy, Loch Oich and Loch Ness.

The geography may have been favourable, but it was not the main reason for the canal's construction. The waterway was one of the earliest examples of a government job-creation scheme. Its purpose was first and foremost to stop the mass exodus of the population from the surrounding area – which, much to the government's dismay, was restricting the supply of conscripts to be pressed into service in the army and navy.

The government hoped that building the canal would stem the emigration; first by creating construction jobs and then, once the canal was completed, by increasing trade in the area. Its confidence seemed well founded. The canal was to be – indeed still is – the first waterway connecting the North Sea with the Atlantic. It was to be broader and deeper than any other canal in Britain, allowing ocean-going vessels to use it, such as those trading with the Baltic states. It would offer ships a safer way to get from one side of Britain to the other than the treacherous Pentland Firth, across the top of Scotland. And, as the final attraction, it would give better protection to Royal Navy ships, in danger of being attacked during the Napoleonic Wars.

So much for the theory. Unfortunately, the Caledonian Canal never lived up to its full potential. It was first proposed as a route in 1773, when James Watt was commissioned to survey it. At the turn of the century Thomas Telford, the veteran road and canal-builder (he was responsible for the Crinan Canal in Argyll too) was appointed principal engineer, on the princely salary of three guineas a day, to carry out the project. He proposed it should be 20ft deep, estimated it would cost £350,000, and take seven years to build.

In fact, it was not completed until 1822 – a full 19 years after the work first started. Its opening was a cause for considerable celebration. In Fort William – which had long harboured grandiose ambitions about developing as a major international port – bonfires were lit, the guns in the fort fired a salute and the local MP held a banquet. The celebrations quickly faded, however. By the time the canal was finished, trade with the Baltics had dwindled, the Napoleonic Wars were over, and larger, more robust ships which could take the Pentland Firth in their stride were already under construction. Just as serious, the canal was only 14ft deep instead of the 20ft proposed by Telford, making it too shallow as well as too narrow for the new, larger steam-driven ships.

In the first few years after its construction, some cargo ships did make the trip through the canal from Glasgow and Liverpool carrying loads of timber, grain and salt. As soon as the canal was opened, it was used to take salted herring from Wick to Ireland. But freight traffic quickly disappeared, and by 1906 it was considered obsolete.

The spectacular scenery, coupled with the novelty of being able to go all the way from coast to coast by boat, did make it attractive to tourists and by 1847 four steamers were regularly plying their trade between Glasgow and Inverness. Such a trip took two days and cost one pound ten shillings (£1.50) for cabin class, and a third of that in steerage. There were also services from Liverpool for a while. In the latter half of the century famous steamships like the *Gondolier* and the *Glengarry* were offering regular trips along the length of the canal, replaced latterly by the *Scot II*, now a floating pub moored near Laggan. The coming of rail and the improvement of roads soon eroded even that traffic, however, and the service between Fort Augustus and Inverness closed in 1930. Nowadays, the traffic is mainly small pleasure craft – British Waterways estimates that more than 5,500 leisure craft used it in 1995, although only about 1,000 boats made a through passage. At popular mooring stations like Laggan and Fort Augustus, you will see large fleets for hire.

About the only way in which the canal did exceed Telford's plan was in its budget. The final cost came in at £912,000, nearly three times his original estimate. Add in the £228,000 cost of deepening the canal just 20 years after it opened, as the government made one last effort to attract traffic, and the cost rose to almost £1.2 million. The over-run was partly due to materials, many of which had to be transported for considerable distances, and whose cost soared during the Napoleonic Wars. Stone had to be shipped up from the Isles of Cumbrae on the Clyde, while bricks came all the way from Liverpool. Even timber – abundantly available now in the Great Glen, but then depleted by shipbuilding, burning and clearing for sheep-farming – was difficult to come by. And landowners like the chiefs Glengarry and Cameron of Locheil negotiated premium rates for their trees. Oak for the lock-gates came from the Baltic; indeed, the gates for the eight locks at Neptune's Staircase are made of cast-iron, sheathed in pine.

Building the canal was not particularly successful in keeping the population at home. At its peak, construction work employed about 1,200 people but finding them was not always easy. Press-gangs were rounding up men for the army and navy; and in the planting and harvesting seasons many preferred to go back and work on the land rather than neglect their crops. Nor was there any guarantee that the money earned would be ploughed back into the local economy. An article in the local *Blackwood's* magazine in 1829 notes: 'Every means were exerted to discourage emigration by providing work for the surplus population . . . of the Highlands and Islands, in particular where the more beneficial system of converting these districts had unavoidably made numerous families destitute.' But, it adds, 'With part of the money received, many hundreds of natives have been enabled to emigrate to our American settlements with comfort and advantage to themselves.'

As a commercial enterprise the canal was never a success. Its accounts show revenues in 1830 of £2,575 against spending of £4,573. By 1856, revenue had almost quadrupled to £9,872 but expenditure had soared to £58,121. Naturally enough, such a disaster demanded a scapegoat to take the blame and consequently Telford was much criticised at the time. But the lack of commercial success was hardly his fault – he was simply doing the government's bidding. And, regardless of the arguments about its commercial value, no one can dispute that the Caledonian Canal is one of the triumphs of British engineering.

Building it tested Thomas Telford's skills to the full. Although it climbs to just 32m (106ft) above sea level at its highest point in Loch Oich, it still needed 29 locks to control the flow of water along its length. Most complex of these by far is Neptune's Staircase with its eight locks, but Fort Augustus, where five gates are needed to get boats down the hill into the town, was almost as taxing. In addition to the locks there are ten bridges, most of them carrying what is now the A82 road from one side of the Glen to the other. There are also weirs to control the water flow and aqueducts and tunnels to take rivers and tracks underneath it.

As if building these landmarks was not enough, Telford also had to change some existing ones. All three of the main rivers which run along the floor of the Glen – the rivers Lochy, Oich and Ness – were diverted to accommodate the passage of the canal. The levels of both Loch Lochy and Loch Ness were raised and Loch Oich, shallowest of the three, was deepened through dredging.

Perhaps the most ingenious repair was made in 1840 at Dunaincroy near Inverness, where it was proving impossible to plug a persistent leak. Thomas Telford's solution was to stick on a giant plaster. Holm Mill, just across the river from the leak, obliged by weaving a web of woollen cloth which was spread over 500 yards of the canal bed. That was covered with layers of 'puddle' (clay, sand and gravel mixed with water) which was then trodden firmly onto the cloth base. One hundred and fifty years later, it still seems to be working.

In 1996, the canal was again closed for maintenance work, this time for refurbishing sills and stabilising some

The aqueduct at Torcastle

of the lock-gates. More work is still needed: British Waterways was recently given a £2.8 million government grant for essential repairs. But the fact that, 170 years after its completion, the canal is still carrying craft from coast to coast is a testament to the skills of those who designed and built it.

The Great Glen Way follows the canal's route from Corpach to Fort Augustus, giving plenty of time to admire the engineering, as well as to enjoy the sight of boats still plying its length.

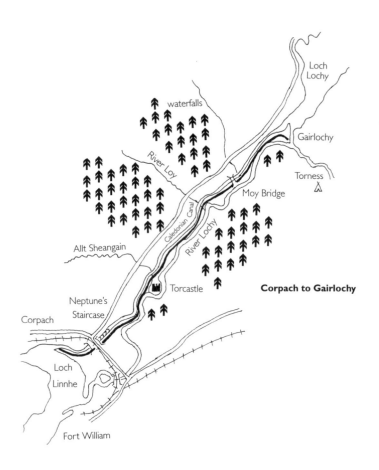

Corpach to Gairlochy

Loch Lochy

waterfalls

River Loy

Gairlochy

Torness

Moy Bridge

River Lochy

Caledonian Canal

Allt Sheangain

Torcastle

Neptune's
Staircase

Corpach

Loch
Linnhe

Fort William

Section 2
Corpach to Gairlochy

You could be forgiven for not noticing it, but you will spend this entire section of the route on an island. The canal towpath which you will follow for the whole 12.7km (eight-mile) walk to Gairlochy is cut off from the 'mainland' by the canal to the north and the River Lochy to the south. It starts at the sea loch of Loch Linnhe and ends at Loch Lochy, the first of the three lochs which form part of the Caledonian Canal.

It is a delightful section. The Way sticks closely to the route of the canal, while the river winds along the floor of the Glen, now hidden from sight, now coursing along close by. The towpath provides easy, pleasant walking, giving plenty of time to savour the dramatic scenery which unfolds from Ben Nevis and Carn Mor Dearg at the start to the gentler and greener slopes of Monadh Beag to the north above Gairlochy. It also contains some of the highlights of the Caledonian Canal, including Neptune's Staircase, the Shangan viaduct and the Moy bridge. By the time you reach Gairlochy, you will be thoroughly immersed in the rhythms and patterns of canal life, the workings of the locks, bridges, weirs and aqueducts.

Corpach basin is an excellent starting place. A popular mooring point for those starting or ending the journey through the canal, there is invariably a colourful collection of boats lining the side of the canal, ranging from leisure cruisers and barges to commercial fishing boats choosing the shelter of the canal rather than the rigours of the Pentland Firth for their journey across Scotland.

Look out, too, for the capstans, the wheel-shaped keys which stand by each lock. The first on the canal stands at the mouth of the basin, a few metres west of the point where the path from Fort William joins the towpath. Until the lock systems were mechanised between 1959 and 1968, the gates had to be opened manually using these capstans. In order to open or close a lock, the wheel had to be turned laboriously seven times. It took three people using poles inserted into the wheel to do this. Now, sailors simply have to ask the lock-keeper to press a button and the gates open or close – a less energetic system, if also rather less romantic.

There are a few shops in Corpach village and it may be worth stocking up on supplies for lunches, snacks and so on. There is a tearoom at Gairlochy, but otherwise there are no shops on the route between here and Fort Augustus, 50km (30 miles) away.

From Corpach basin, the Great Glen Way heads along the south-eastern bank of the canal, past a long avenue of tall sycamore trees and into the Great Glen. As you leave behind the last few houses of Caol, the flat expanse of Corpach Moss and the Blar Mor open up on the left. It is from here that the district of Lochaber (derived from the Gaelic word *aber* meaning 'marsh') may have taken its name. Now well drained and crisscrossed by roads and railways, there is evidence that there was once a small lochan in the middle of the Moss.

Across on the other side of the canal are the workings of a disused quarry, one of a number in the area to take advantage of the schists and granites from which the hills are formed. As you leave Caol behind, the urban scenery is quickly replaced by one of the finest views in all

Scotland: the massive bulk of Ben Nevis with its intimidating buttresses and gullies looming over the deep Coire Leis. Consider yourself lucky if you can see the summit – it is clear of mist and fog for an average of just 60 days a year.

Soon, the eight locks known as Neptune's Staircase come into view. From this angle, it is hard to imagine that boats could possibly climb such a steep slope. For a closer look, go through the kissing gate where you meet the first of the ten swing bridges on the Caledonian Canal. They are now opened automatically by the bridge/lock-keeper, but when the canal was first built they had to be operated by hand. Cross the railway track

Neptune's Staircase at Banavie

taking care to listen out for trains heading along the Mallaig to Fort William line.

As you cross the line, you bid farewell to the railway system until you reach Inverness. Despite a variety of enterprising but ultimately doomed attempts to establish a rail service through the Great Glen, it has never been possible to get from Fort William to Inverness by train. Immediately after the railway is the bridge across the road to Mallaig. Cross the road, again taking care as it can be very busy in the summer, and go through the gate which leads back on to the towpath.

You now have a grandstand view of Neptune's Staircase, one of the most spectacular engineering features on the canal. It is a fascinating place to linger a while and watch the boats negotiate the climb. The eight locks raise the canal by 19m (64ft) in just 450m (500 yards). Completing the climb takes a boat about an hour and a half – a far easier passage now that the lock-gates are automatic than in the old days of hand-operated capstans. Then, it took a full 126 complete turns of the capstan's pole to get from top to bottom. In the heyday of the canal, boats were crammed into the locks as tightly as possible so that as many as possible could make the climb in one go.

Construction of the Staircase alone cost £50,000, far more than Thomas Telford had estimated, reflecting the soaring cost of materials during the Napoleonic Wars. The large white house across on the other side of the canal is the original lock-keeper's house, now a listed building. The bow windows are characteristic of canal buildings; they were designed so that the occupant could easily see both ways along the canal to check for approaching vessels.

The top of the Staircase is a good place to stop and

watch the hustle and bustle as ships negotiate the Staircase. Banavie is a popular mooring spot and there will usually be some boats to inspect as you wait for the lock-gates to turn. A shop is advertised in the buildings on the right as you reach the top of the Staircase, but its opening hours are erratic and it would be unwise to rely on it.

Continuing along the towpath, you quickly leave the hustle and bustle of Banavie behind. The towpath here is lined with a variety of trees, oak, hazel, rowan, alder and fir among them. Further along towards Gairlochy, there are a few fine examples of the old Caledonian pine on the opposite bank. Combined with the yellow and green of the gorse and whin which line the canalside, the towpath is a brilliant splash of colour whatever the season. The gorse and whin may brighten the scenery, but they are actually there to serve a practical purpose. Most of the bushes were planted by Telford and his canal-builders to bind the sides of the banks. Judging by the remarkable resilience of the canal walls, they continue to do a good job.

The further you walk from Banavie, the more rural the scene becomes. Houses are fewer and further apart and the hills on either side of the Glen become more visible. Ben Nevis and Carn Mor Dearg on the right are soon joined by the smooth, rounded slopes of Aonach Mor, its ski paraphernalia littering the slopes. Rather less intimidating are the hills on the left: Meall Bhanabhie which, in its Anglicised version, gave its name to the village of Banavie, and, further ahead, Monadh Beag marks the start of the Great Glen proper.

This was a bumper section of the canal for aqueduct-builders. While the rest of the canal gets by without a single one, the 9km (six miles) from Banavie to

Gairlochy boasts a grand total of four, three of them large enough to walk through. The first of these comes just after the canal turns briefly eastwards and takes the Banavie Burn underneath it to the River Lochy beyond. You need not linger too long here, as better examples lie ahead at Torcastle and Loy. Soon after crossing the burn are the ruins of a smallholding, large and impressive enough to suggest it was once a rather grand residence, then the canal veers northwards again.

Here, you get the first sense that you could be walking on an island. The river approaches close by on the right, leaving just a narrow strip of land between it and the canal to carry the towpath. The experience is brief, however. The island quickly widens as you approach the area known as Torcastle, named after the castle once occupied by Banquo, Thane of Lochaber, around the tenth century, and, as Shakespearean scholars will know, general and confidant of the murderous Macbeth. Little remains of the castle now but it is worth making a detour to the site to enjoy the views of the River Lochy. Rather uninspiring though it may seem from the towpath, at Torcastle the river is transformed into a delightful waterway, complete with small pools and waterfalls and surrounded by a delightful variety of trees and shrubs. How wise of Banquo to choose this site.

It was home to the MacIntoshes of Tor Castle until the end of the 13th century, when they moved off to Badenoch. Eighty years later, it was seized by the Camerons, who made it their family seat until 1660 when it was replaced by Achnacarry House, which lies by the side of Loch Lochy further ahead on the Great Glen Way.

A detour to visit it also gives you the chance to inspect the second of the Caledonian Canal aqueducts, the

The ruins of Torcastle

The River Lochy from Torcastle

Shangan aqueduct, which carries the Allt Sheangain through to the river. It is well worth locating even if you do not carry on down to Torcastle. To get to both of them you should take the path which climbs down the

54

bank just as you reach a couple of houses, known as the Torcastle cottages. The steep path reaches the bank of the river just as it emerges from the aqueduct. Looking back towards it, you get an excellent view of its three tunnels, two carrying water and the third allowing animals and pedestrians to cross to the other side of the canal. You may like to walk through, but take care: the bricks are slippery and the tunnel is very dark in the middle.

To continue on to Torcastle itself, head down the track away from the aqueduct to a farm gate on the right. Go through the gate and follow an indistinct path through the trees, keeping Allt Sheangain on the right. Where the burn flows into the River Lochy, turn left and carry on through the trees until a mound, with the castle perched on top of it, appears ahead.

It is a lovely, peaceful spot. Situated on a bend of the river, the views in both directions are spectacular, with trees dipping over the banks and the rocks creating a series of delightful pools. The castle itself has all but disappeared, swallowed up by the trees and shrubs which surround it. The few sections of wall which remain are a haven for colourful plants like tormentil, saxifrage and heathers. A little way beyond the castle, an avenue of beech trees along the riverbank is still known as Banquo's Walk, marking the spot where he liked to stroll.

The deepest pool below the castle is known locally as the Cat's Pool, in honour of the escapades of the 12th Cameron chief, Allan nan Creach. By all accounts a rather nasty and power-crazy man, he spent much of his time raiding his enemies and seizing their lands. Rather unexpectedly struck by remorse during his later years, he consulted the witch Gormshuil to ask how he could atone for his sins. She ordered him to go through the ordeal known as Tan Ghairm, which involved lighting a huge fire on the banks of the Lochy, constructing a large spit and ordering his servant to roast a cat on it. The victim's yells soon drew the attention of his fellow felines, a string of which turned up at the door of Allan's house to warn him: 'This is ill-usage for a cat.' Allan reassured them that 'all will be better presently' until one particularly large, fierce cat appeared and threatened to tear him limb from limb unless he released the poor roasting creature. Allan agreed on condition that the cat king tell him how he could atone for his misdeeds.

The cat king ordered Allan to build seven churches around the area, one for each of his misdeeds. Allan agreed and told his servant to free the cat, whereupon it leapt for relief straight into the river, taking the other cats with it. Allan proceeded to build his churches, three in Lochaber, one near Loch Laggan to the south of the Great Glen and the others further west at Knoydart, Arisaig and Morven. The one nearest here was at Kilmallie, probably close to the road of the same name which the route goes along at Corpach. No trace of the building remains.

Retrace your steps to the towpath and turn right to continue to Gairlochy, savouring the view of Monadh Beag and the occasional glimpses of the higher hills which lie ahead on the north-west side of the Glen. The dense green of the commercial plantation which lies on the left bank of the canal contrasts sharply with the rich variety of trees and shrubs which characterised the woods around Torcastle. The Forestry Commission is becoming more sensitive to the need to vary its plantations and there should be fewer monotonous tracts of trees in the future. That will not only make the commercial plantations, which are so vital to the Scottish economy, more pleasant to look at and walk through, but also more attractive to the native plant and wildlife.

The island narrows once again as Torcastle is left behind, giving views to the broad stone bed of the River Lochy as it courses through the Glen. The third aqueduct lies in this narrow section, on a curve in the canal in the centre of the Dubh Chlaise forest. It takes the River Loy from Glen Loy into the Lochy. Connoisseurs of aqueduct architecture claim it is the finest of the three, so why not climb down to the bank to view its tunnels and decide for yourself.

Through the aqueduct lies Glen Loy, scene of one of the most famous marches in Scottish history. Bonnie Prince Charlie came down Glen Loy with more than a thousand loyal clansmen after he had raised his standard at Glenfinnan. From here, it was virtually a straight road all the way to the celebratory ball at the Palace of Holyrood House in Edinburgh.

At the bottom of Glen Loy lies Errocht House, once the home of a branch of the Cameron clan. Bed and breakfast accommodation is available from the farm a little way back along the B8004, and Glen Loy Lodge, a little way up the Glen, also offers rooms.

Back on the towpath, the route is an almost straight line to Gairlochy. The trees thin out, emphasising the flatness of the flood plain as it stretches across the river and beyond towards the towering hills. Soon, the distinctive white bars of the Moy swing bridge come into view – another piece of the canal's history. Officially known as a Double Leaf Swivel Bridge, Moy is the last remaining accommodation bridge (so called because they allowed livestock to pass from one side of the canal to the other) on the canal. Once all nine were operated like it, but the others were mechanised in the 1930s. This one

The canal as it approaches Gairlochy

was left as a reminder of how the canal originally worked. Built in north Wales and transported north, it was erected at Moy in 1821. Instead of swinging open in one uniform movement as the rest of the canal bridges do, the two halves of this bridge have to be opened separately. That means the bridge-keeper has to open one half, then get into his boat from his cottage on the eastern side and row across the canal to the west side to open the other half. Just as well the traffic on this bridge is light!

From here, it is a short stroll into Gairlochy. Again, the river encroaches quite close on the right, its wide, stone-strewn bed giving it almost a coastal feel. Cross a weir which drains excess water from the canal into the Lochy and head on along the path, past the avenue of trees into Gairlochy.

To call Gairlochy a village would be to greatly overestimate its status – it has only a few houses, a telephone box, a bridge and two locks. More welcome for walkers, it also boasts a tearoom. It may be small, but Gairlochy is all the more charming for that. The dramatic green of the trees which line the canal as it flows into Loch Lochy is the perfect foil for the white of the well-preserved buildings and the lock-gates. The tall, white building is the old lock-keeper's cottage, a twin of the one in Banavie. The room at the top of the house, with the characteristic bow windows, is still known as Telford's Room as this was where he liked to stay when he came to inspect the progress of his canal workers. His visits, by all accounts, were sociable affairs.

The son of a shepherd from Dumfriesshire, Telford started life as a stone-dyker in his native county before working his way up from labouring to become one of Britain's finest engineers. Before being commissioned to build the canal, he was best known for the roads and bridges he had built, although he also constructed the Crinan Canal. He was a popular man with his labourers and bosses alike. He would sit smoking and chatting with his navvies over drams of whisky, but it was said that he always kept a needle, thread and button ready to make running repairs to the one suit he wore on his travels so that he would always look respectable.

Landlords welcomed Telford's custom. One of the best-known anecdotes about him concerns the Ship Inn, where he stayed on his frequent trips to London until his friends, concerned that he should have the comfort of a place of his own as he grew older, arranged accommodation for him. When the Ship's recently installed landlord heard this news he was aghast. 'But I have just paid £750 for you' – the additional price paid for the inn on the promise of the business Telford would bring. Gairlochy has plenty of examples of the great engineer's skills.

The canal now follows the route once taken by the river. The latter's course was diverted through the Mucomir Cut, a short walk down the B8004 towards Spean Bridge, where it starts with a spectacular waterfall now harnessed for the power station there. It is worth strolling a few hundred metres down the road towards Spean Bridge to see the Cut and hear the thunderous falls as they plunge down from the source of the River Lochy.

It was here that Bonnie Dundee, one of the heroes of the first Jacobite rebellion, raised an army drawn largely from the clans Donald, Cameron, Stewart and McLean. Intent on regaining the Scottish crown for King James, Dundee recruited local men and marched south to Killiecrankie, where he defeated King William's men – but only at the cost of his own life. His death effectively ended the brief rebellion and his men returned home.

Fifty-five years later, the area saw the first blood to the Scots of the '45 rebellion at Highbridge, just south-east of here. On the road built by General Wade as part of his programme of bridge- and road-building, a party of soldiers making their way from Fort Augustus to strengthen the garrison at Fort William was ambushed and taken captive. Three days later, the hostages were paraded in front of Bonnie Prince Charlie as he raised his standard at Glenfinnan.

Gairlochy has plenty of colourful history to think about as you rest awhile. If you want to stay the night, however, the choice of accommodation is limited. There is a campsite a little way up the B8004; otherwise, you will have to carry on to Forest Lodge or the bed and breakfast next to it, near the junction with the main A82, or into Spean Bridge four miles east of Gairlochy.

Such a diversion would have the advantage of taking you past the Commando Memorial, a monument to those who trained for action in this area during the Second World War and whose escapades are outlined in the next section.

Bonnie Prince Charlie

Lochaber used to be known as the Cradle of the Rebellion, a testament to the role its clans played in the Jacobite struggle to restore the Stuarts to the monarchy. All along the route of the Great Glen Way you will encounter landmarks and tales of the glories and tragedies of the Jacobite Rebellion, a past that is much more than the names of tea-shops and hotels.

Much of the drama of the Jacobite risings of 1690, 1715 and, most famously, 1745 took place in and around the Great Glen. Many in the army which marched with Bonnie Prince Charlie to Derby in 1745 were drawn from clans in and around Lochaber. And his escape from Culloden back to France was made possible only by the support of the clan chiefs of the Great Glen who were willing to hide him on their land, to provide him with food and clothing and to carry the messages which eventually got him safely on board a French ship.

If Lochaber was the cradle, the Camerons could claim to be the hand that rocked it. When Charles Edward Stuart landed at Loch nan Uamh on board the *Le du Teillay* on 25 July 1745, determined to restore his father, the uncrowned James VIII to the throne (Jacobite comes from Jacobus, the Latin for James), he summoned Donald Cameron, the Gentle Locheil and the clan's 19th chief, to ask for support. Locheil, with warnings from his colleagues ringing in his ears, set out determined to tell the Prince to return to France. Instead, he was won round by the Prince's pleas, his allegiance guaranteeing the support of hundreds more wavering clan members.

That guarantee of support was enough to give the Young Pretender the confidence to raise his standard, signifying his determination to reclaim the land he believed rightfully belonged to his family. At 5 p.m. on 19 August 1745, with 1,200 clansmen gathered around, the red and white silk flag of the House of Stuart was flown at Glenfinnan, almost due west of Achnacarry at the end of Loch Shiel, as Charlie declared himself Prince Regent and his father King. Thus began an eight-month campaign, which ended ignominiously with defeat at Culloden and a further five months as a fugitive from the bloodthirsty Duke of Cumberland.

The historian T. Ratcliffe Barnett describes the moment in *The Land of Locheil and the Magic West*: 'Much has been written about the folly of the Great Adventure that began when a handful of fools, as so many saw them, raised their standard at Moidart but all who admire the spirit of adventure and understand the thrill of the luck of the gambler's throw will understand how this glorious tragedy came about.'

The Prince's campaign started promisingly enough; just a month after raising the standard, Charlie had captured Edinburgh, having marched east through the Great Glen and south across the Corrieyairack Pass to Perth and then Stirling, unchallenged by government troops. Four days later, the Highlanders, now swollen in number to more than 2,500, trounced General Cope's men at Prestonpans and began the long march south towards London.

That they only reached Derby, 130 miles from London, before opting for retreat is variously blamed on the weak will of Charlie's key lieutenants, defecting Highlanders or the might of the English forces ranged against them. Certainly, the Prince's advance had London worried; the Bank of England had even started paying out only in sixpences to prevent a run on its funds. But almost 30,000 government troops lay between the Highland army and London, with the English led by such trusty soldiers as the King's brother Cumberland and General Wade, and Charles could muster only 5,000 men – some of them hankering to return to the Highlands – although he was confident he would pick up support from the Welsh and French as he approached the capital.

Instead, his lieutenant-general, Lord George Murray, advised retreat and, after a long and bitter council of war, Charles was outvoted. So, on 6 December, the long march home began. Despite victory over General Hawley's troops at Falkirk, the chiefs recommended that Charles return to home territory in the Highlands. Inverness was easily recaptured from the government forces and the Prince spent two months there, pretending he was the conquering hero. In the meantime, however, Cumberland's forces were approaching from the south.

Then the Prince made the fatal mistake of his campaign. He assembled his 6,000 troops on Culloden Moor, an open stretch of land south of Inverness, completely unsuited to the Highland method of hand-to-hand combat. To make matters worse, Cumberland did not attack on 15 April as the Prince expected, celebrating his 25th birthday at Nairn instead and feeding and watering his 9,000 men in the process. The Jacobites, meanwhile, huddled on the moor with only a biscuit apiece for sustenance.

Vengeance for the mistake was swift. It took just 25 minutes on 16 April 1746 for the Highland army to be destroyed, with more than 4,500 of them left dead and dying on the battlefield. Charles himself escaped down the Great Glen, reaching Invergarry Castle at two o'clock the following morning. The next day, he reached Glen Pean at the top of Loch Arkaig and waited for news of his vanquished army. The 1,500 survivors had gathered at Ruthven at the end of the Corrieyairack Pass and there was plenty of ill-feeling against the Prince. He realised the campaign was over and sent a brief message to Ruthven: 'Let every man seek his safety in the best way he can.'

The Prince's own escape was long and tortuous. He headed first for Borrodale where the French ships had

Loch Arkaig

deposited him just eight months earlier; but when no help arrived and the government troops grew threatening, he fled over the sea to Skye. There, he missed the French ships which rescued many Jacobites and narrowly avoided capture and, with the aid of Flora MacDonald, escaped back to the mainland. After almost three months of wandering, including two weeks hiding in caves in the Dark Mile between Loch Lochy and Loch Arkaig, he heard of French ships at Loch nan Uamh, the spot where he had triumphantly landed the previous year. He quickly fled across Lochaber to the beach and on 19 September, with rather less ceremony, left Scotland for France.

Vengeance on the clansmen continued, however. The experience of Donald Cameron and his brothers was typical. The Gentle Locheil died in exile in France. One brother, John – who opposed the rising and deliberately stayed away from the house whenever the Prince spent the night there – was hounded for nine years until the government found an excuse to banish him from Scotland in 1755. He remained in exile for ten years. Alexander, another brother, was a Jesuit priest who had converted to Catholicism and became the Prince's chaplain. He was captured after Culloden and died on a prison ship on the Thames while awaiting transportation. A third brother, Archibald, was a doctor who became the Prince's adviser and physician to the troops. He escaped to France but, having returned to the Highlands to continue the campaign, was betrayed and in 1753 was taken to the Tower of London where he was hung, drawn and quartered – the last man to die for the Jacobite cause. The only brother to escape punishment was Euan, and that was only because he had emigrated to Jamaica.

Dedicated treasure hunters can dream of finding their own personal share of the Jacobean legend. The last battle of the rebellion was at sea, by Loch nan Uamh, when three government gunboats were sent off to attack French ships carrying supplies to the Jacobites. The British failed to capture the invaders, and a cache of 30,000 louis-d'or was hidden on the shores of Loch Arkaig. The clan chiefs say the money has all been accounted for but local legend has it that some remains.

The Cameron museum at Achnacarry House on the next part of the walk includes a section on Bonnie Prince Charlie and the rebellion. There is also an extensive exhibition, including a number of his personal

Along the shore of Loch Lochy

belongings and other artefacts, at the folk museum in Fort William. Both are worth a visit to find out more about the truth and the romance of Scotland's greatest adventure.

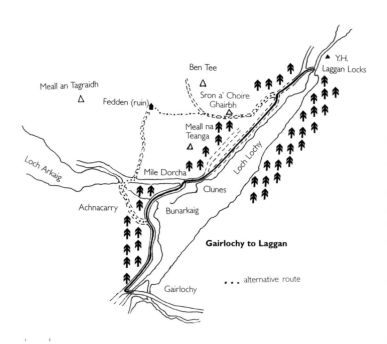

Meall an Tagraidh
△

Ben Tee
△

Fedden (ruin)

Sron a' Choire
Ghairbh
△

Meall na
Teanga
△

Y.H.
Laggan Locks

Loch Arkaig

Mile Dorcha

Loch Lochy

Achnacarry

Clunes

Bunarkaig

Gairlochy to Laggan

Gairlochy

• • • alternative route

Section 3
Gairlochy to Laggan Locks

You are now entering Cameron country. For most of this section, you will be walking on land owned by the Locheil, chief of the Clan Cameron since the Scottish people first organised themselves in family groups. Do not be surprised if you hear the skirl of pipes or catch a glimpse of the swing of the kilt as you stride through the trees. In the land of Locheil, it is impossible not to remember the Great Adventure in which the Camerons fought alongside Bonnie Prince Charlie in his daring bid to recapture the Scottish crown for his father.

The scenery of this section is most appropriate to the romance of the story of the rebellion. From Gairlochy onwards, the walls of the Great Glen will gradually close in, leaving a narrow corridor which runs almost all the way to your destination at Inverness. This section also includes the first loch of the Glen: Loch Lochy, long and narrow and bordered on either side by dramatically swooping hills and tall trees. It is all too easy to imagine fugitive clansmen hiding in the forests, escaping across the towering hills or taking to the water in their small, silent boats, with the King's men baying at their heels.

If you want to experience the thrill of fleeing through the hills, or simply like the idea of getting into the open country, there is an alternative high-level route for the middle section. While the Great Glen Way sticks to the loch shore, walking mainly on forest tracks, the alternative goes up to the shores of the beautiful Loch Arkaig, fringed by hills and the site of some of the greatest mysteries of the '45 rebellion. From there it heads into the hills, climbing through one of Scotland's finest mountain passes before rejoining the main path. None of the walking is difficult (although there is one small section where the path becomes indistinct) nor is the climbing too strenuous. But it should only be tackled if you have experience of hillwalking and know how to use a map and a compass. Even the safest of hill routes can become treacherous to the inexperienced if the mist descends.

You will be immersed in the forest almost as soon as you leave Gairlochy. From the canal path, head across the bridge towards Achnacarry, savouring the views of Ben Nevis and the Aonachs, some of the finest on the Way. At the other side of the bridge, turn right along the road which winds along the shore of Loch Lochy.

The blueprint for the official Great Glen Way proposes a new path through the forest which will then run along the loch shore until just before Achnacarry House. At present, however, it is too difficult to fight through the trees and across the ditches and bogs which lie in the forest, so take the B8005 road instead. What the route loses in seclusion it gains in ease of walking, giving plenty of time to enjoy the glimpses of the loch and the surrounding hills which gradually open up after Gairlochy. The road is quiet even on the busiest summer days so the traffic should never be heavy enough to be too much of a hazard.

For a short distance, the loch shore is obscured by the delightful mixed forest. Trees like oak, birch, alder, and ash line the shores of the loch, which can be seen glinting blue through occasional small clearings. Further along the route, they are joined by magnificent tall pine trees and sitka spruce which loom high above their smaller neighbours. A similar pine and birch forest on the south-west shore of Loch Arkaig is thought to have been there since the last Ice Age and it is not hard to imagine that these mighty specimens are descendants of a long-established forest.

The loch comes dramatically into view about 2.5km (1½ miles) along the road, when a clearing in the trees reveals a broad expanse of water ahead. This section of the loch, where it curves into a wide bay at the mouth of the River Arkaig, is the widest. Its end remains hidden from view around the headland at Clunes.

The very steepness of the hills on this side of the loch means that you cannot really appreciate their height; the tops of mountains like Meall na Teanga and Sron a' Choire Ghairbh, the Great Glen's only two Munros, and their slightly smaller neighbours Ben Tee and Meall Odhar, are largely hidden from view. Instead, your eye will be drawn to the smaller (but still dramatically steep) slopes across the water like Leitir Fhoinnlaigh and Beinn Iaruinn which lies just behind it.

The road continues to climb and dip gently, sticking close to the loch shore. On the left, the Gray Mare's Tail – seemingly Scotland's favourite name for a waterfall – tumbles down the slopes of the Monadh Beag. Shortly, the road turns inland and approaches the tall gates of Achnacarry House, home of the Cameron clan chiefs, which is steeped in history almost as much as the clan itself.

The Camerons first made their home at Achnacarry in 1660, when a house was built there to replace Torcastle on the River Lochy. The first Achnacarry House was destroyed in 1746 by the Duke of Cumberland to punish the Camerons for helping Bonnie Prince Charlie – the Gentle Locheil returned wounded from Culloden just in time to witness the flames engulfing it. The remains of the old house can just be seen by the side of the River Arkaig near the present mansion. The house was rebuilt in 1802 and has seen as much of the excitement of battle as its predecessor did, albeit in a different way.

Two hundred years after it was occupied by Cumberland's men, British troops again took possession of Achnacarry, but this time with the Camerons' blessing. From 1942 until the end of the Second World War, Achnacarry housed the Commando Basic Training Centre. Every new recruit to the Commandos, some 25,000 in all, had to pass through the centre before they could earn the legendary green beret. It took some earning.

Achnacarry quickly became known as one of the toughest training centres in the world. The terrain, climate and demanding regime devised by Lieutenant-Colonel Charles Edward Vaughan, who commanded the centre from its inception until the end of the war, would have ensured that alone. But, to recreate real battle conditions, the recruits also used live ammunition which, sadly, meant that some men were killed before they had even completed their training.

The toughness of the regime was obvious to the commandos as soon as they arrived at Spean Bridge railway station. A kilted pipe major welcomed them off the train, where their kitbags were loaded onto lorries. Those expecting to follow their equipment into the trucks were soon disabused of such soft notions; their first assignment was to march the seven miles to Achnacarry House. When they got there, they were greeted by a row of mock graves marked by white crosses which lined the path between the castle and the guard-room. Each was inscribed with warnings such as: 'He failed to keep his rifle clean' or 'He showed himself on the skyline' – fictitious, of course, but pointed enough to inspire fear in these raw recruits.

Lt.-Col. Vaughan made full use of the inhospitable territory which surrounds Achnacarry House to school the recruits in survival and guerrilla tactics. Sometimes they would be braving the currents on Loch Lochy to cross in their small boats from Bunarkaig to Glenfintaig on the other side of the loch. Or they might be white-water canoeing on the fast-flowing River Arkaig or risking life and limb on the Death Slide and Tarzan courses on the estate. Those who wanted to get away from the house could always stretch themselves with an 18-mile run to the foot of Ben Nevis, a quick ascent of the 4,406ft peak then back again – all in a day's work.

The house itself did not survive the war unscathed. A fire, appropriately enough on 5 November 1943, destroyed part of it. That did not stop the commando trainers, but it was part of the reason the house was rebuilt after the war. The current building dates from 1952 and is nowadays occupied by the 26th Cameron chief, Sir Donald Cameron of Locheil. No trace of the exploits of the commandos remains, although a leaflet available from Fort William tourist information office helps identify the location of some of the more famous training courses. It is worth a detour up to the house, both to enjoy the beauty of the woods surrounding it and to visit the Clan Cameron Museum opposite. As well as giving a history of the Camerons, it has some photographs and memorabilia of the commando training centre. The museum, housed in a picturesque whitewashed building which was the old post office, is open in the afternoon between spring and autumn, and by arrangement at other times.

The memorial at Spean Bridge honours the Commandos who trained at Achnacarry

Achnacarry House also has the dubious distinction of being the last place where the pit and gallows were used by clan chiefs to punish cattle stealers and deter others from the same crime. The right of the chiefs to use the gallows was removed after the '45 rebellion, but some carried on for a few years after that.

If you do decide to visit the museum, you may like to return to the route via Loch Arkaig and the Dark Mile rather than simply retracing your steps. This is also the start of the high-level alternative for this section, described more fully at the end of the chapter. Outside the museum, turn left away from Loch Lochy and follow the road up to the white metal bridge (built by some of the commandos stationed here). The views of Loch Arkaig from here are breathtaking. The still water reflects the purples, oranges and greens of the heather- and bracken-strewn hills, the trees which surround it

softening its shore. Small wonder that Queen Victoria, who sailed in a steam yacht up the loch on a visit to Achnacarry in 1873, was moved almost to poetry. 'I feel a sort of reverence in going over these scenes in this most beautiful country, which I am proud to call my own,' she noted in her journal, 'where there was such devoted loyalty to the family of my ancestors, for Stuart blood is still in my veins, and I am now their representative and the people are still as loyal and devoted to me as they were to that unhappy race.'

A part of the forest is an unusual memorial to Bonnie Prince Charlie. The Gentle Locheil was planting a row of beech trees when he heard that the Young Pretender had landed at Glenfinnan. In his hurry, he planted them all in a cluster, expecting to return soon to thin them out. In fact, the year of advances and retreats which led to the defeat at Culloden, followed by Cameron's exile in

The Witches' Cauldron and Cia-aig Falls

France, meant the hastily planted trees grew to maturity without thinning.

Cross the bridge and walk along the end of Loch Arkaig to the B8005. Turn right to return to Loch Lochy. A little way along the road, a hump-backed bridge –

78

much used in commando training – marks the site of the delightful Cia-aig waterfall. The pool at the bottom of the fall is known as the Witch's Cauldron, and is so-called because of a tale of cattle poisoning and intrigue.

A number of Cameron's cattle were afflicted by an unusual sickness which no amount of ministrations by vets and farmers seemed able to cure. Suspicion fell, as suspicion did in those days, on an old crone who lived near the shore of Loch Arkaig. Some of the clansmen went to investigate but upon entering the house found no trace of the old woman. There was only a hissing, wild-eyed striped cat there. Too clever to be fooled by such dodges, the men bundled the cat into a sack – after much clawing and scratching – and carried it off the Cia-aig, where they threw it in. Just as the sack hit the water, a shriek arose and the cat transformed itself into the shape of the old woman. She died and the cattle were miraculously cured.

These days, the only magic woven by the pool is its bewitching beauty, with the clear water tumbling across the rocks and the beautiful birch, oak and rowan trees reflecting in its waters. It is a delightful place to linger over a late breakfast or mid-morning snack. In the trees above here, Bonnie Prince Charlie hid in a cave for two weeks after his flight from Culloden. Once marked on maps, it is now all but hidden behind trees and shrubs. The high-level alternative to Laggan starts by climbing the path at the side of this waterfall. Full details are given at the end of the chapter.

Carry on down the Mile Dorcha or Dark Mile, so called because of the beech trees which used to crowd both sides of the road, long before it was laid with tarmac and given a classification. If you are feeling tired, spare a thought for the poor commandos. The first speed march for trainees was a five-mile round trip from Achnacarry House along the Dark Mile, laden with battle gear but moving together as a complete unit. The task was to complete it in just 50 minutes!

The canopy of trees which gave the road its name is long gone; while there are numerous small beech trees, interspersed with rowan, oak and pine, it is now no darker or more mysterious than any of the other roads on the Way. The old walls on the right have the distinction of being a site of special scientific interest because of the rare mosses which line its stones and boulders.

Much touted as a great scenic attraction, not all the Dark Mile's visitors have been impressed. Robert Southey, the poet, complained: 'It is not such as this appellation would lead a traveller to expect.' Indeed, it is likely that the building of the road, and the tree-felling which that required, removed the road's original beauty. It is a pleasant walk nonetheless, and you can always amuse yourself by searching for hints of the escapades the Dark Mile saw during the '45 rebellion. As well as the cave above the Witch's Cauldron, Bonnie Prince Charlie is also believed to have taken refuge first in a tree, long since blown down. When the road reaches the loch and goes sharply right, turn left and continue towards the forest.

Those missing out on Achnacarry House should continue along the road round the bay to Bunarkaig. This is a glorious spot; there are views down Loch Lochy towards Gairlochy, with the massive bulk of the Grey Corries looming behind. In the foreground, the scenery is brightened by rhododendrons, a brilliant splash of colour in early summer. The River Arkaig, although at less than a mile long one of the shortest rivers in Britain, is also delightful, tumbling here through a granite gorge towards the loch. If you really succumb to the charms of the spot, you can camp – ask permission from the estate cottage by the bridge.

Just before the bridge is a small building, now used as a kennels complete with noisy dogs. Cross the bridge and continue along the road towards Clunes. Note the giant Sequoia trees along the side of the road, an incongruous sight among the copses of pine, ash and beech. The road leaves the loch shore and cuts across a marshy area. The large white house on the left is a private hostel for Cameron Boy Scouts.

Instead of going along the Mile Dorcha, turn right down a forest track past a few small holiday lodges and a carpark. In the summer, there is also a small shop and hut offering cycle hire. The official route proposed for the Great Glen Way takes the high road along the side of the loch. At the moment, however, that track ends abruptly at a gorge about two-thirds along its length and you have to scramble down a bank strewn with the debris from tree-felling in order to join the lower path. It is easier to carry on along the cycle track which hugs the loch shore. To do that, take the right-hand fork after the carpark and continue along the path through the forestry plantation. Almost immediately, a path forks off to the right and heads down to the loch shore. This is a good place to stop and enjoy the views of the loch, but the road to Laggan lies straight ahead.

The tall conifers which make up the forest clearly identify it as a commercial plantation, but the track through it is wide and there is enough variety of trees to make this a pleasant walk. The dense green of the trees is also an excellent backdrop for the blue waters of the loch, which you will be able to glimpse regularly through the clearings in the forest. Birds of prey soar overhead, among them buzzards, sparrow-hawks and even the occasional golden eagle straying from its more usual haunts in the high tops. Nor is the forest too dense to block out ground vegetation; primroses, harebells and various other flowers brighten the path in season.

The track winds along the loch shore, passing through three high wooden gates erected to protect the trees from the deer which you may spot along the way – probably by their white tails bobbing nervously as they flee from your approach. As well as the red and roe deer which are common in Scotland, the Great Glen is also home to Japanese sitka deer, which were introduced on the shores of Loch Ness in 1900 and have since spread along its length. There is some concern that inter-breeding will lead to the eradication of roe deer and their replacement by a hybrid sitka species.

As the path emerges from the forest into a clear-felled stretch, look behind you to your left. From here, you get a grandstand view of the Great Glen's two Munros – Meall na Teanga (hill of the tongue), whose rounded top lies slightly behind you, and Sron a' Choire Ghairbh (nose of the rough corrie), which faces it across the pass. Called after Sir Hugh T. Munro, who first chronicled them, Munros are hills with summits above 3,000ft. In all there are 277 of them, and bagging them is now one of Scotland's national sports. You can join in if you wish by spending an extra day at Laggan and strolling back to bag Sron a' Choire Ghairbh. The route is described at the end of this chapter, along with details of the alternative high-level route which gives you a close-up view of the two hills, without the effort of getting to their summit.

Continue along the path, noting the remains of a ruined bothy, Glas-dhoire, on the right-hand side – what a view to wake up to every morning! Across the loch, you can see the buildings of Letterfinlay, once home of a branch of the Cameron clan. Tales of the parsimony of the MacMartins, reputedly the oldest branch of the Locheil family, are legendary. A visitor one wet spring day, observing the rainwater gushing through the roof, asked MacMartin why he did not repair the thatch. 'Who the devil would think of thatching a house on a day like this?' was the retort. The two men met again in the summer, when the sun was beating down. The visitor commented that it seemed a good day to make repairs to the roof. 'Who the devil needs a roof on a day like this?' he was told. Another tale concerns a traveller, desperate for rest and sustenance. Having knocked twice on MacMartin's door to no avail, he finally called in despair: 'If there be a Christian in this house, surely he will let me rest a while within?' MacMartin's reply was swift: 'There are no Christians here, we are all Camerons!' His parsimony paid off, at least for his descendants; when he died, £500 was discovered under his pillow – a princely sum then.

The path winds upwards then levels out as another track joins it from the left. This marks the place where the high-level alternative rejoins the Great Glen Way. Continue along the path, across a cattle grid and through a gate which brings you onto a tarmac road down to Laggan Locks. By now, the white buildings of the lock are clear at the end of the loch, looking very attractive against the backdrop of trees and hills. Carry on past some holiday chalets and grazing land towards Kilfinnan Farm. Through the farmyard, going towards the shores of the loch – called Ceann Loch in this section – lies the walled ground of the Kilfinnan cemetery. The large structure in the centre is a mausoleum of the chiefs of Glengarry.

Cross the Kilfinnan Burn and continue down the road until you get to a second holiday park with wooden chalets. Turn right past the chalets and walk across the head of the loch, along a causeway bounded by the loch on one side and a marshy bog to the other, to reach Laggan Locks. This was the site of one of the oddest-named battles in Scottish history. Fought on a baking hot day in July 1544 between the Frasers and the massed ranks of the MacDonalds, Camerons and MacDonnells, who were returning from an expedition in the west, the heat was so intense that all the men removed their plaids and fought in their undershirts. Since then, the tussle has been known as Blar Leine, or Battle of the Shirts.

It reputedly started because Ranald Galda, heir of Clanranald but brought up by his grandfather among the Frasers, visited Castle Trim to assert his rights. So appalled was he by the feast got up in his honour that he chastised his hosts as they slew seven oxen with the comment: 'A few hens would have served just as well.' His clansmen immediately christened him Ranald of the Hens and suggested he take his meanness back to the Frasers. Whatever the truth behind the battle, neither side could be said to have emerged well from it. The Frasers were almost wiped out and the other side fared little better. A plaque commemorating the fight lies just at the eastern side of the loch, although the actual site is now probably under water, swallowed by the loch after Thomas Telford raised its level to accommodate the canal.

Perhaps the strangest tale about the battle concerns its aftermath. Legend has it that all the Fraser men killed in the battle left pregnant wives. All, reputedly, produced male children. The story is supported by the fact that in July 1564 when Lovat was made governor of Inverness

Castle, he had 80 men with him, all about the same age, and all of whose fathers were killed in the Battle of the Shirts 20 years previously.

The view down Loch Lochy and back along the route from the locks is magnificent. The two Munros are at their majestic best and the tree-lined banks of the loch taper gently as the water narrows. It is also a good spot for boat watching; Laggan is a favourite starting point for cruises on the Caledonian Canal and there is likely to be a bustle of sailors and boats approaching along the loch, or passing through the lock-gates.

Laggan has a tearoom and a pub on a boat, the *Scot II*, both open in season. The *Scot II*, an impressive-looking boat which used to take tourists up and down the Caledonian Canal in its heyday, now stays moored at Laggan. There is a variety of guest-houses and bed and breakfast places on the main A82 road. To reach them, walk along the track by the plaque commemorating the battle instead of continuing along the canal. The youth hostel is best reached by staying on the Great Glen Way until the weir is reached a short walk further on.

High-level Alternative

Those who want to get among the hills may like to try an alternative route to Laggan. It takes you through a magnificent high Scottish glen, around some dramatic mountains and through spectacular scenery. Although more taxing than walking along forest tracks, the route is not over-demanding for a reasonably fit walker. The mountain pass does climb to more than 700m (2,300ft) but the slopes up to it are relatively gentle. For the most part, it sticks to clear paths apart from one short section in the middle, where you will have to pick your way across featureless moorland which can be wet at times.

Having said all this, the route should not be tackled lightly. You must have a detailed map of the area – Ordnance Survey Landranger sheet 34 is recommended – and experience of using maps. While the paths are mostly clear, it would be easy to stray off them in poor visibility, so you should carry a compass and be confident you can use it to navigate your way out of difficulty. You should also carry spare clothing, waterproofs and basic food supplies in case the weather deteriorates rapidly.

It is a splendid walk, and well worth doing for those with some experience of hillwalking. To start it, follow the route to Achnacarry House, described earlier in the chapter, continuing past both the house and the museum and on past the old stables. Cross the bridge and continue along the edge of the loch, even more beautiful for being all but deserted, until you reach the B8005 which continues part of the way along the loch.

Turn right, away from the loch, and walk down the road for a few hundred yards until you reach an old stone bridge at the bottom of the Cia-aig waterfall. Here, the route starts to head upwards into the open country. Take the path up the side of the waterfall. It soon veers away from the river so that you will not see the water again, only hear its roar, until high in the glen. Climb the clear path on the eastern side of the falls, heading into the trees. The thick commercial forest is a shock after the delightful mixed trees around Achnacarry House, but the trees are far from oppressive and the atmosphere cool and pleasant on even the hottest summer days. The layer of needles underfoot provide a pleasant carpet to cushion the feet as you start the climb.

After about 30 minutes' steady climbing, the path joins a broader forest track. Turn left and head up it towards Glen Cia-aig. The coniferous trees now thin out and are interspersed with a variety of deciduous species. The more height you gain, the more the views open up to the hills above Loch Arkaig as well as to the peaks ahead which will dominate the landscape for the rest of the day's route.

The track turns gradually north-east and heads into the wide sweep of Glen Cia-aig. Far down on the left is the Cia-aig Burn, now glimpsed only occasionally through the trees as it tumbles in a series of small falls down the hillside. It will gradually climb up to meet the path again at the head of the glen.

The path starts as a clear Land Rover track with an easy gradient, giving good walking through the wide Glen. This track ends before long and is replaced by a small path which continues through a wood, still coniferous but smaller and more mixed than the commercial forest you left behind at the falls. Numerous small burns tumble down the slopes of Meall Breac, often bordered by clumps of mountain ash and hawthorn – all of which make delightful places to rest and contemplate the scenery. In places, there are planks to help you cross the burns, but these can be tricky to negotiate when the burns are in spate; take care after heavy rain.

The forest track may be narrower than the Land Rover road, but it gives easy walking nonetheless. It meanders gradually up and down, through thicker trees and occasional clearings, heading always for the broad hump of Meall an Tagraidh which stands guard over the end of the Glen. This area is a haven for birdlife; as you walk along you may spot the distinctive black and white plumage of the stone chat. In the more open moorland ahead, grouse and pheasant may lumber from the ground as you pass, disturbed from their torpor, while dotterels leap with much more vigour, chirruping merrily to alert others to your approach. Deer, too, are common in the Glen. In the winter and early spring, you may see them on the broad moorland, foraging for food. In the summer they retreat up the slopes to graze on the grass and heather.

The forest ends abruptly at a fence designed to keep the deer out but which is now rather dilapidated. A high and rather rickety stile crosses the fence – take care while crossing it. The path continues, growing fainter in places, on the other side of the fence. Soon, it takes you to a wooden bridge across the Cia-aig. Upstream, the water tumbles over rocks and through little gorges while the

Looking towards the col

banks of the burn are lined with small trees, all of which provides a delightful contrast to the sparse moorland round about.

You are now truly in open moorland; barely a tree will disturb your views until you are well over the pass and on your way down to the south Laggan forest above Loch Lochy. Heather and marsh grasses, interspersed with mountain flowers are all around. In the spring, this is also a favourite spawning ground for frogs. Frog spawn congeals in most of the little pools and puddles you will pass, and small greenish frogs will leap at your feet should you pass too close to their hiding places. This should give you a clue as to one of the possible hazards of this stretch of the walk: bogs. It can be very wet

underfoot, although the path steers clear of the worst of it.

As the path winds round the bottom of Meall an Tagraidh, the col between Meall na Teanga and Sron a' Choire Ghairbh, which you will cross to rejoin the Great Glen Way, comes into view. It is tempting to take the most direct route and head directly across to it, but that would mean descending quite a long way only to have to climb up again at the other side. Not only is that effort unnecessary, it is also the spot where any surface water will linger, so the going is likely to be wetter than on the high ground. More sensible is to head round the glen to the ruined buildings of Fedden and then cross the glen floor from there.

Fedden is a stark reminder that the Highland glens

The ruins at Fedden

were not always as deserted as this. Glen Arkaig once had a sizeable population, whereas nowadays there are only sheep and deer there. The same is true in countless other Scottish glens. Hard though it may be to believe as you survey the deserted countryside, some inhabitants were driven out by over-population: the land was not rich enough to support the numbers trying to make their living from it. Others were forced out by shepherds from the south and from England who rented the land from clan chiefs. They had decided that sheep and deer were more profitable tenants than crofters and forced the people from their traditional lands.

Last, but by no means least, Highlanders were forced out during the clearances, the brutal punishment wreaked against them in the wake of their defeat at

Culloden. Perpetrated nowhere more enthusiastically than at Fort Augustus by the notorious Duke of Cumberland, many thousands lost their lands, watched their houses burn down and their cattle destroyed by English soldiers. No one can calculate accurately how many were driven out of the Highlands by these varied forces.

William T. Kilgour, writing in 1908 in *Lochaber in War and Peace*, summed up the effects: 'It is somewhat pathetic nowadays to wander through these desolated glens; there is a pathos in the ruined homesteads – a requiem in the breeze and even the waves on the beach, lapping unceasingly, seem to croon dolefully for the stalwarts that have passed away.'

Long abandoned though it may be, Fedden is a spectacular location for a house. From here, the view to the south looks almost alpine, while off to the north-west you can pick out the serried ranks of the hills stretching from Glen Quoich, the next glen along, and beyond to the Glen Shiel ridge. It's enough to make you resolve to return to sample the other delights of the area once the Great Glen Way is completed.

From the ruined buildings, it is best to carry on along the path a little before branching right to cross the floor of the Glen. It means you can keep to the higher ground and you will be able to pick out the drier areas by following the line of green grassy areas rather than the brown peat hags. In less than 20 minutes, you should be across the floor of the Glen and searching for the path which winds round the bottom of Sron a' Choire Ghairbh on the other side. The path is a little way up the slopes and, if you cannot identify it immediately, keep winding round the hill toward the col where you will find it as it rises to the pass between the two hills.

The path continues all the way to the col and beyond. While it may look a long distance and a steep climb away, do not despair. The gradient of the path is gentle and the going not too challenging. The top of the col is likely to be the windiest spot of the day, as whatever breeze there is funnels through this low point in the mountain wall.

From the col, you will see Loch Lochy again, glinting blue far below, and across to the hills at the other side. Compared to those close by, they look positively tame. The highest of the Great Glen's hills, Meall na Teanga, can be clearly seen to the south, its long swooping summit curve looking something like the tongue which gives the hill its name. The summit of the other Munro, Sron a' Choire Ghairbh, is above the col to the north, but is hidden from view by the steepness of the approach. If you feel energetic, a route up it is described in the next section as an excursion from Laggan.

From the col, head down the path towards the loch. It is a deceptively long climb down, but is pleasant nonetheless. The trees gradually thicken and become almost exclusively coniferous as you approach the loch.

The path ends at a forest track where you turn left and continue along towards Laggan. After about two miles, a path comes up from the right to meet the main track. This marks the spot where you rejoin the Great Glen Way and you should follow that route for the short walk into Laggan.

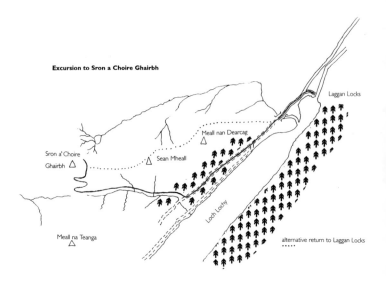

Excursion to Sron a Choire Ghairbh

Laggan Locks

Meall nan Dearcag

Sron a' Choire Ghairbh

Sean Mheall

Loch Lochy

Meall na Teanga

alternative return to Laggan Locks

Excursion 1
Sron a' Choire Ghairbh

If you have always wondered why there is so much fuss about Munro-bagging, this excursion is for you: Sron a' Choire Ghairbh is a great introduction to the joys of the sport. It is a straightforward, fairly gentle climb (in comparison to other Munros) to the summit. Once there, the views all around are grand – not only both ways along the Great Glen but also north towards Glen Shiel and south across the Monadhliath hills towards the Cairngorms and the hills above Loch Tay. And, of course, there are excellent views to the magnificent hulk of Ben Nevis and its neighbours.

Those who have already sampled the joys of Munro-bagging will need no encouragement to undertake this excursion. After all, how could you be in the Great Glen and not tackle at least one of its two Munros? Indeed, dedicated baggers will no doubt also take in the other, Meall na Teanga, situated conveniently close by, weather and time permitting.

Munro-bagging owes its existence to Sir Hugh T. Munro, a physician born in 1856 in London. A keen walker and one of the earliest members of the Scottish Mountaineering Club, he took it upon himself to chart all of Scotland's hills over 3,000ft (915m). He identified 283 of them but subsequent, and often controversial, revisions have reduced that number to 277. Some traditionalists still prefer to stick to Munro's original tables.

Since the Revd A.E. Robertson became the first person

to complete all the Munros – sadly Munro himself was thwarted by the dread Inaccessible Pinnacle in the Cuillins of Skye – Munro-bagging has been elevated to a national sport. Thousands have followed in the reverend's footsteps, some of them knocking them all off in one season – even in the winter. Variations of the sport have also included bagging them on mountain bikes and climbing them in order of height – particularly frustrating when, as on this excursion, two or more of quite different heights are separated only by a col or section of ridge.

To start the walk, retrace your steps from South Laggan across the canal, past the holiday chalets and back along to Kilfinnan Farm. While the Great Glen Way went along the loch shore, this route takes the high road through the forest. At the point where the road forks shortly after the second cattle grid, take the right-hand track instead of heading down towards the water. Walk along the forest track until just before the woods become more mature and the trees taller; at this point, the Corriegour Lodge lies directly on the other side of the loch.

Look for a small wooden bridge on the right-hand side of the track. Cross this to a set of steps climbing up to a path which winds steeply, first through the trees and then out through a gate into the high, narrow glen. At certain times of the year, the path is used by shepherds taking their flocks to and from the moorland which lies beyond the col. It is a marvel to watch them controlling the animals with just a couple of dogs and some brief signals. Approach them carefully: sheep scattered by inconsiderate walkers can take the shepherd a long time to gather again, and will not endear you to those who make a living from the hills.

The Allt Glas Dhoire

The Allt Glas Dhoire hurtles down through the glen towards the loch. A waterfall can be seen through the trees, and its sound will accompany you for a large part of the climb. You quickly leave the forest behind and pass into open countryside, the transition marked by a gate through the fence built to protect the new trees from deer. Now the burn tumbles down a series of steps, stark against the heather-covered banks of the steep-sided Glen. High on the hills, crags jut out and the occasional solitary rowan tree clings precariously to the steep slopes. The path is steep but clear, quickly reaching the first staging-post – Cam Bhealach, the U-shaped col which marks the start of the paths up to the Great Glen's two Munros. Near the col, the path becomes less steep and the ground more grassy. The path also becomes less distinct but is still easy enough to follow up to the col, where it once again becomes well trodden. A cairn marks the route near the summit of the col – useful for those descending in poor visibility.

A rest stop will be welcome after the long climb from the loch, and where better to choose than here. From the top of the col, a high mountain glen unfolds to the west, fringed with row upon row of hills – see how many you can identify. To start you off, the one directly ahead is Meall an Tagraidh, and further away are the peaks around Loch Arkaig. Directly to the south is Meall na Teanga, twin of Sron a' Choire Ghairbh, the destination of the excursion, its summit still concealed behind the steep slopes above.

To start the final ascent, take the path which goes steeply northwards from the col. It is a well-made path and the long zigzags take some of the effort out of this last climb. The climbing ends on a broad grassy ridge where the path all but peters out. The route remains clear, however; the summit is left along the ridge. A small cairn on the ridge marks the best place to start the trek to the summit, which lies about 300m (1,000ft) further on. Here, the views to the west are joined by equally splendid ones to the north and south, the massive bulk of the Aonachs still visible at the end of the Glen.

The return is by the same route as the ascent, so retrace your steps back to the col and down the path into the forest. Experienced walkers may want to try a different route back to Laggan, which continues along the ridge and drops down to the road close to Kilfinnan Farm. There is no path and the route involves negotiating your way round small hills, rocky outcrops and down the steep slope above Laggan. It can be difficult, particularly in poor visibility or bad weather, and should only be undertaken by those confident of their ability to pick out a route.

This alternative descent starts from the cairn which marks the top of the path up from the col. Instead of taking that path, continue along the ridge as it dips and climbs, across a subsidiary peak called Sean Mheall, towering high above Loch Lochy. The ridge dips, then rises again to Meall nan Dearcag, the knoll which marks its end. Do not climb this final hill, but instead go left and circle round its northern flanks. Although this is a less direct route than climbing straight over the top of Meall nan Dearcag, the slopes below that hill are rocky and steep, making the descent dangerous. The slightly longer route will be both quicker and safer. Keep as high as possible while circling the hill. The slopes around the Allt a' Choire Ghlais are rather steep, and end in a waterfall just above Kilfinnan – not an advisable descent. Keep instead well to the east and

THE GREAT GLEN WAY

above the river until you are just above the farm and graveyard, then climb carefully down through the fields. Rejoin the track just above the farm and continue back to Laggan.

A word of caution for anyone considering the route. Although Sron a' Choire Ghairbh is one of the easiest Munros to climb, with clear paths all the way, it is still a serious hillwalking expedition. Do not tackle it unless you are carrying detailed maps of the hill and surrounding area and have the proper equipment, including stout boots, warm clothing and waterproofs. In poor weather, you should not climb it at all unless you are skilled in mountain navigation. Inclement weather is a lot more severe on the hills than at sea level; the winds will be stronger, the rain heavier and the temperature much lower. Mist can descend on sunny days, making even the most familiar of terrain confusing. There are numerous corries and cols just off the paths and ridges on Sron a' Choire Ghairbh which could be dangerous to stray close to. Always take a compass and make sure you know how to use it. Do not even think about tackling the hill in winter unless you are an experienced winter walker and have an ice axe, crampons and the other winter walking equipment. In summer, remember to take plenty of water – dehydration can be a real problem in the hills.

Having said all that, with careful preparation and the right equipment, it is a delightful climb. Go well prepared and you will come back satisfied – and yet another convert to the thrilling sport of Munro-bagging.

Alongside the 'cut' at Laggan

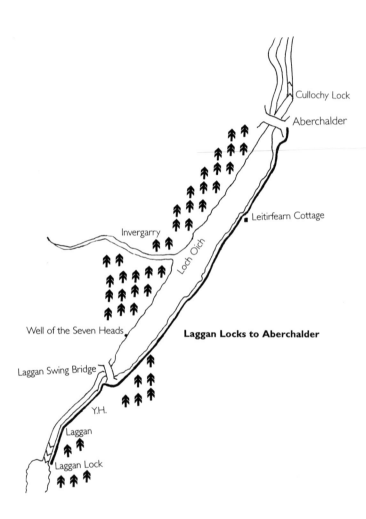

Cullochy Lock

Aberchalder

Leitirfearn Cottage

Invergarry

Loch Oich

Laggan Locks to Aberchalder

Well of the Seven Heads

Laggan Swing Bridge

Y.H.

Laggan

Laggan Lock

Section 4
Laggan Locks to Aberchalder

This is one of the prettiest sections of the Great Glen Way. It starts with a stroll along the short section of canal which joins Loch Lochy to Loch Oich, the smallest and most picturesque of the Great Glen lochs. It then continues through the Leitirfearn nature reserve, a delightful stretch of forest which nestles below the hills on the secluded south-east side of the loch.

Like Loch Lochy, the shores of Loch Oich are lined with trees. In contrast to the commercial plantations of the previous section, however, the trees in the Leitirfearn reserve are varied and native, their contrasting colours, sizes and shapes making a pleasant backdrop to the beauty of the loch itself. This is also one of the quietest sections. Apart from a brief spell on the road at the beginning, you will be walking in splendid isolation, along little-used paths, some way from the nearest traffic – apart from the boats, of course.

As you set off, admire the views down Loch Lochy for a final time then turn and head down the towpath, keeping the canal on the left. Walk past the *Scot II* and the other boats which are moored here until you reach the wooded section. Leave the towpath on a path which forks off to the right just as the trees start and climb on to the top of the spoil bank, constructed from the wastes of canal-building. The canal bank on this section is badly eroded and it would be very easy to fall in, so it is best not to try to continue at the lower level. Besides, the views of the canal and the trees on the other bank are far better from this slightly higher vantage-point. Forming what is known as Laggan Avenue, the trees around here were planted by Thomas Telford to provide timber for maintenance on the canal, but they long ago stopped being felled for that purpose. That is to our benefit: the forest is a delightful mixture of native species such as rowan and ash as well as some imported varieties like cypress, beech and pine.

The wood is a haven for birds, and you may see warblers and long-tailed tits among the variety which dart through the trees. The woods of Laggan Avenue also encourage far more mixed vegetation than the commercial forests by Loch Lochy. Look out for the wonderful colours of tormentil and willowherb, and the rich variety of heathers. The rampant rhododendron is much in evidence, its shiny green leaves providing an attractive backdrop to the bright clumps of flowers which adorn its branches in early summer.

On the right is the small stone church built for the canal workers by Thomas Telford. Whether it was popular or not is unknown, but it's odds on that after a hard day's work many of the navvies sought solace in the pub rather than the pew. Although the building of the canal was seen as a way of creating work for the Scots (and thus stemming the tide of emigration), in fact many of the workers were Irish rather than Scottish. The word navvies derives from navigators – the name used to describe those who built Britain's system of navigations, including its canals and waterways. Their skill is clear from the fact that the banks they built more than 170 years ago are still holding back the water.

The church is a tiny, undecorated building. Inside, a plaque carved with five heads is a touching memorial to the five sons of the local landlord who all died in infancy.

The story is told that when the laird converted to Catholicism he was cursed by a local witch who declared that his family would never have a male heir. To this day, so the tale goes, the curse has proved accurate and the family's wealth has passed through the female of the line.

The path meanders through the trees and bushes, with occasional glimpses down into the dark waters of the canal and beyond to the fields and moorland which edge the Glen. It comes to an abrupt end at a weir which takes the Allt an Lagain into the canal. A slight detour is needed to get round it. Turn right and walk along the brick wall of the weir down to the A82 road. From here, it is a short stroll back to the Laggan youth hostel and a couple of other places offering bed and breakfast, including the friendly Forest Lodge.

Laggan was formerly known as Feith Drum and was the site of the annual Ridge Fair, where deals were struck, legal affairs settled and justice meted out at the Stone of the Ridge. For the ultimate punishment, there was the gallows tree, which stood at what is now the site of the youth hostel.

Climb up the bank again at the other side of the weir and continue along the path to Laggan Bridge. This section is rather overgrown and, if the bushes and briar defeat you, you may prefer to stick to the road for the short walk up to the swing bridge. It will not be pleasant walking. The cars come quickly along this stretch of road and the verges are narrow; take care particularly when lorries or buses pass. Laggan swing bridge, at 106ft above sea level, marks the canal's highest point. This milestone is marked by the flow of water changing direction. Until now, the lock-gates have opened westwards, to allow the water to flow down to Fort William and the Atlantic. At the other end of Loch Oich, as you will see when you reach Cullochy Lock, they open eastwards to take the water to the North Sea beyond Inverness. This does not, however, mean the Great Glen Way is downhill all the way from here; the high point of the walking route has yet to come, and there are three steep climbs to get through as the route heads away from the Caledonian Canal beyond Fort Augustus.

Those with a taste for the bizarre may want to take a detour a little way beyond the swing bridge to a monument half a mile away. Tobar nan Ceann, or the Well of the Seven Heads, commemorates the Keppoch murders. Although the story of the incident is written in Gaelic, French, Latin and English below a carving of seven heads, the four languages make it no easier to understand the reason for the killings.

The bloody massacre was sparked by the deaths of two members of the Keppoch family following a dispute between them and another branch of the clan, the MacDonnells, over succession to the chieftainship. Although it was claimed that the deaths were an accident, Iain Lom, the famous Keppoch bard, did not believe the story and spent two years trying to drum up support for retaliation. He eventually persuaded a MacDonald chief from Skye to get involved and, with the help of some of the Skye clansmen, slew the seven murderers in their home in 1663. With a grand sense of drama, he then cut off their heads and took them to the local Glengarry chief, who had refused to get involved in the fight, stopping to wash the heads in a well at this site on the way. The well has vanished but this monument, erected by the 27th chief of Glengarry in 1812, remains to remind us of the bloody deed.

The Great Glen Way heads right before the bridge, down a track which leads to the Great Glen Waterpark.

Walk past the holiday chalets towards the Leitirfearn nature reserve. Just at the start of the forest is a stretch of wall which marks the platform of Invergarry station, one of the stopping points on the Fort Augustus to Spean Bridge railway. It closed long before Beeching started swinging his axe in the early 1960s, but is still much lamented. These days it is difficult to pick out the landmarks which identify station buildings; once, however, it was a rather grand affair. The station itself was built in the style of a Swiss chalet, complete with verandah and a private waiting-room for the occupants of Invergarry House – who, of course, would not want to mingle with the other travellers. Passengers would probably also have been able to contemplate the magnificent fir tree which can still be seen at the end of the platform; judging by its size, it was there long before the railway track was built.

The next section of the route follows the path of the old railway; just as the station has all but vanished, so too there is now little sign of the old tracks. The history of the Invergarry and Fort Augustus Railway Company is sad and salutary, its untimely demise owing more to ill-placed pride and lack of common sense than to any inherent disadvantages with the route. General Wade and Thomas Telford ably demonstrated the suitability of the Great Glen for communications, and it seems equally well suited to rail travel.

The saga had its roots in a long-running feud between the North British Railway Company (which ran the trains to Spean Bridge and Fort William), and its rival, the Inverness-based Highland Railway Company, both of which wanted to run a rail connection along the length of the Great Glen. The rivalry between them had successfully thwarted their ambitions until a third company – the Invergarry and Fort Augustus Railway Company – applied for, and won, planning permission to construct a track to Fort Augustus in 1896. Not surprisingly, the old rivals were none too pleased with the young upstart, particularly when they heard it planned extending the service all the way to Inverness. The Highland Railway cleverly disguised its displeasure with enthusiasm, offering to co-operate with the little Invergarry and Fort Augustus company to get trains right to Inverness (although its real motive was, of course, to keep its North British rival out) and even agreeing to operate the line on the Invergarry's behalf. On the strength of these deals, the Invergarry invested heavily, buying enough ground for a double track and building viaducts and tunnels and even a pier and station at the end of Loch Ness, the remains of which can still be seen from Fort Augustus.

The Highland's co-operation, of course, turned out to be fictitious; indeed, it cut 30 miles off its own main line service to Inverness to ensure Invergarry passengers remained stranded in the Glen.

The result was predictable. The Invergarry and Fort Augustus Railway Company got into serious financial difficulties and was forced to close its station at Fort Augustus. Next, the Highland withdrew its support. The North British reluctantly came to the Invergarry's aid but it was too late, and the company abandoned the line in 1911. The first-ever public campaign against railway closure got it reopened two years later, but the reprieve was short-lived. By 1933, passenger services had been withdrawn and in 1946 it finally closed for good. As you admire the scenery on your walk along the disused line today, you can imagine how spectacular it would look viewed from a railway carriage.

The Leitirfearn forest is one of the finest examples of ash, elm and hazel woodland in the country, and deserves its status as a nature reserve. It is certainly a beautiful walk, with the delightful variety of shapes, sizes and species of tree providing a perfect barrier against the dense commercial plantations which lie above it on the hill, almost out of sight. The glimpses of the loch as it glitters silver through trees, the carpeting of mosses and lichens, the sprinkling of flowers like enchanters nightshade, wild iris and, in late spring, carpets of bluebells, all combine to make this a lovely section of the Great Glen Way. Small waterfalls tumble down the hills through viaducts and tunnels built to channel the water away from the railway. The path is little used and cars are kept safely away on the other side of the loch, so the quietness of this stretch also makes it a haven for wildlife. Birds such as blackcaps, wood warblers and tree pipits and occasionally even buzzards can be seen. Nesting boxes have been placed by the side of the path to encourage pied flycatchers and redstarts to breed.

The area is not just rich in birds, but has abundant animal life too. The forest is full of deer – which, if disturbed, have been known to take to the water to make their escape. Deer are not normally known for their swimming skills, but if you are lucky enough to catch sight of a mature stag forging its way strongly across the water to Invergarry, you will quickly change your mind.

The Great Glen Way only follows the railway track for about 15 minutes, at which point it becomes too overgrown to continue. At the high fence, now entwined with the glossy green leaves of rhododendron bushes, which was constructed to divert walkers from the railway, take the steep path which leads down to the left. It joins an old military road, part of the network built by

General Wade, which goes along the shore of the loch. Immediately on reaching it, cross the high stile which takes you into the Aberchalder estate.

Soon, the remains of Invergarry Castle appear across the loch. Once the seat of the MacDonnells of Glengarry, the rock on which it stands gave the clan its war cry: Creagan Fhithich or rock of the raven. Like many of the Great Glen's castles, the ruins you see here are not the first building on this site; at least two earlier strongholds had previously existed here as part of a string of forts and castles designed to give strategic control of the Glen. This one was built in the early 16th century and, according to local legend, the stones for its construction were taken from Ben Tee and passed from hand to hand for seven miles to the site of the castle.

Glengarry's empire was extensive, although not perhaps as widespread as he liked his servants to think. One, a stalker called Alasdair Dubh, wanting to impress a traveller he'd met on Coire Glas above Loch Lochy said: 'All that you see is Glengarry's, and all that you do not see, that too is Glengarry's.'

When needed to rally to the clan's cause, Glengarry's men were summoned by a beacon lit on Creag nan Gobhar, the hill which lies directly behind you, which is known today as Glengarry's beacon. A fiery cross on the castle ramparts was the signal to light the beacon.

The castle was used as a garrison for English troops for 23 years, from 1692 to 1715, after Glengarry apparently surrendered to them. He won it back after a siege in 1715, writing a letter to the governor of the Fort William garrison to boast of his success. Like the rest of the Great Glen chiefs, Glengarry was a supporter of Bonnie Prince Charlie. Indeed, the Young Pretender twice stayed in the castle, once as a guest on the eve of his triumphant march across the Corrieyairack Pass to Stirling, and again on his flight from Culloden. Then, he arrived at two o'clock the morning after the battle and Ned Burke, the Gaelic-speaking Highlander who acted as his guide, cooked salmon to give him sustenance for his onward journey.

Glengarry's reoccupation was short-lived. When the rebellion collapsed after the Battle of Culloden, Glengarry again surrendered himself to the English, who took their revenge by burning the castle. The inhabitants were herded onto a nearby hill and forced to watch while, as Kilgour puts it, Colonel Clayton, on his way to Skye: 'burnt the sawmills of Invergarry, plundered the poor people's houses, stripped women and children and shot their cows, besides taking without payment what victuals he wanted and carried off their horses'.

The castle was briefly occupied in 1727 by Thomas Rawlinson, head of the York Building Company which started a smelter in Invergarry, producing iron known as Glengarry pigs. The company soon failed and Glengarry returned to the castle. His clansmen, however, were evicted from their homes during the clearances and their land given over to sheep-farming. Most stayed loyal to the clan even in exile, including those who settled in Canada, where they continued the Highland traditions. There are now more Glengarry MacDonnells in Ontario than there are in the Great Glen.

Paradoxically, the Glengarry Castle Hotel, which stands just along the loch from the old castle, was built by Canadians who emigrated to the Great Glen. Before it became a hotel, it was the principal mansion of the Ellice family, who had made their fortune from the Hudson Bay Company and other business ventures in Canada and the United States. The Ellices were the driving force behind the building of Invergarry, which

Leitirfearn Cottage

began as a classic planned village in the style so beloved of the Victorians, complete with school, laundry, hospital and corn mill. Most of these buildings remain today, although many are now private houses.

As you continue along the military road, you will see the green and red buoys which mark the navigable channel along the loch. As well as being the smallest of the Great Glen's three lochs, Loch Oich is also the shallowest at just 50m (164ft) at its deepest point. To make it navigable by boats using the canal, part of the loch had to be dredged. The markers pinpoint the deepened area. During the dredging, a number of oak trees dating back to prehistoric times were found on the loch bed, and for this reason it is still referred to as Loch Sticks by trawlermen.

Small and shallow though it may be, Loch Oich still has many attractions. It is the loveliest of the three lochs on the route. You will have a chance to see this for yourself when the shore curves to create a small headland

112

on the left-hand side of the path just by the tiny whitewashed Leitirfearn Cottage. Walk down to the shore here and look in both directions along the loch for some of the finest views on the route. If you look carefully, you will see evidence of Invergarry's main surviving industry: power generation. The concrete walls visible on the other side are not a landing jetty but the outflow from Invergarry power station, well concealed behind the trees and the island.

From the cottage, the path starts to climb steeply to cross a bridge over the railway. Looking down at the workings of the tunnel, you cannot but admire the complexity of the crenellated pillars and other stonework on the bridges. It's a pity that they did not put the same effort into making the enterprise a commercial success! The military road then drops again at the other side of the bridge and continues over the Calder Burn via a four-span railway bridge.

Cross the river on the bridge and continue along the shore of the loch as it narrows gradually on the approach to Aberchalder. The path here is indistinct initially, but if you go through the gate on the left immediately after the bridge and walk along close to the shore, you will pick up a path which leads along to the towpath as you approach the swing bridge.

From the loch shore, there are fine views back along Loch Oich to the hills behind. This spot is a favoured nesting place for herons as well as a winter grazing area for deer. Aberchalder Farm, east along the A82 road, offers bed and breakfast, as do some of the other nearby cottages in summer.

113

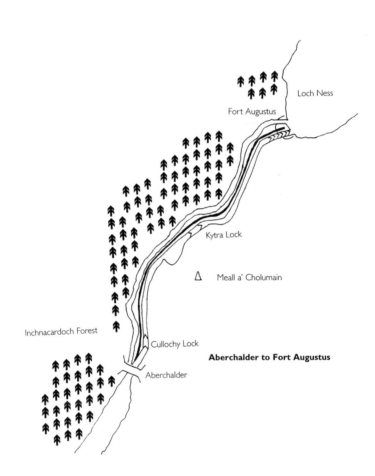

Loch Ness

Fort Augustus

Kytra Lock

Δ   Meall a' Cholumain

Inchnacardoch Forest

Cullochy Lock

Aberchalder

Aberchalder to Fort Augustus

Section 5
Aberchalder to Fort Augustus

You are about to discover one of the Great Glen's best-kept secrets, namely the stretch of canal between Aberchalder and Fort Augustus. From Cullochy Lock, with its selection of bridges, through Kytra Lock, the quietest and prettiest on the whole route, to the long, gentle descent into the bustle of Fort Augustus, this 8km (five-mile) stretch is one of the highlights of the entire Way. You may be walking along a man-made towpath beside a canal, but it will feel like one of the most idyllic of natural rivers; you may stay within a kilometre or two of one of the main roads across Scotland, but traffic and the bustle of crowds will seem a million miles away.

The canal meanders through the Glen, hardly needing to be bounded by walls and towpaths. The hills surrounding the path are high and close enough to give a feeling of scale to the landscape, yet far enough away to ensure that you do not feel closed in. The mixture of natural and commercial forest plantations gives a delightful variation of colour and texture to the hills, while the farmed fields bounded by bracken-covered moorland lend the landscape a pastoral feel.

Once more you will be walking on a narrow causeway, this time between the canal and the River Oich. As in earlier sections, the river will be glimpsed only occasionally; for most of the route, it is hidden below the banks of trees on the left as you head towards Fort Augustus. You might be able to hear it, however; in spate, the current can be quite fierce. Its route was diverted near

The old Oich bridge at Aberchalder, built by James Dredge

Fort Augustus, where the riverbed was used for the canal.

This section of the Great Glen Way starts at Aberchalder swing bridge, but it will not be that bridge – similar to the three already met on the route – which will catch your eye. Instead, your attention will focus on the Bridge of Oich, the suspension bridge which carried cars across the River Oich until the new bridge was completed in 1932. Built in 1850, it was designed by James Dredge, an engineer from Bath. Now dilapidated and unused, it is still an impressive structure, and far more pleasing to the eye than the bridge in current use. The remains of another old bridge, this one built by General Wade for the princely sum of £50, can also still be seen at Cullochy.

Cullochy was the last lock to be built on the new waterway and was not completed until after the official opening of the canal in 1822. The delay probably owed something to the delicate negotiations with MacDonnell of Glengarry, who owned the land on which the lock was to be constructed, and who was determined to extract the maximum price possible for selling it and allowing access rights to the canal-builders. Doubtless he argued sentimental value; it was in the fields around here that his ancestor gathered his clansmen ready to march with Bonnie Prince Charlie for the '45 rebellion.

Like many of the original canal buildings, Cullochy Lock is a scheduled ancient monument and a most attractive spot. Looking back, you can see down through the Glen to Loch Oich, with Ben Tee beyond, offset by the broad expanse of the fen around. Looking ahead, the water reflects the glorious array of colours from the trees and hills round about.

The Great Glen Way sticks to the north-west towpath for this section, so cross the bridge to reach the towpath and turn right on to the canal bank. Continue along the towpath past Cullochy Lock from where the causeway broadens to become like a small island. Note the direction of the locks: they open to the east to allow the water to flow towards the North Sea – all the others encountered up to here had opened westwards, draining to the Atlantic.

Ahead on the left is the dense dark green of the Inchnacardoch forest, the first plantation to be bought by the Forestry Commission shortly after it was founded in 1919. Lord Lovat, who sold it to them, became the first chairman of the Commission. One section of the forest was for years used as a nursery, the saplings transplanted from here to create forests across Scotland and beyond.

Soon, the canal broadens out to become more like a narrow loch than a canal. Telford concluded that the lie of the land was such that an embankment on the east side was not needed. That gives this part of the canal a very natural feel, and the shoreline is varied and tree-lined instead of uniformly straight and bound with gorse as on much of the rest of the waterway.

Above the shore to the east, a television mast pinpoints the summit of Meall a' Cholumain. Although it is not very high, the hill is a superb vantage-point, giving excellent views along the entire length of the Great Glen. That makes it well worth climbing for anyone completing the Great Glen Way, and a route to the top – a gentle half-day walk – is described at the end of this section.

The peace and natural tree-cover makes this area a haven for wildlife. Birds like yellowhammer, chaffinch and redstart and even bats, in the fading light of day, have made their homes around here. The wildflowers and bushes also attract butterflies and dragonflies which hover here in profusion during the summer.

Beyond the bank on the other side of the canal the trees thicken into a small copse and, as you approach Kytra Lock, there are some spectacular tall pines. On the hill to your left as you reach the lock are the remains of an Iron Age fort, Torr Dhuin, on a promontory at the edge of the forest. Dating back more than 2,500 years, the fort is yet another indication of the strategic importance of the Great Glen. One of the many along its length, these prehistoric hill forts were usually built on the ice-resistant rock which made them useful as vantage-points. The route will pass close to Craig Phadrig, near Inverness, the most famous hill fort in the Great Glen.

Cross a weir between the canal and the river, which can be rather wet underfoot at times, to reach Kytra Lock. It is the prettiest on the canal and you should make use of the well-situated picnic tables to stop and admire the view. Surrounded by trees and set against the backdrop of Beinn a' Bhacaidh and the other hills which lie to the south-east of Loch Ness, the white-painted lock-keeper's cottage is very picturesque. Those who know the hidden beauties of the canal use this spot as a mooring place but it is quieter than the more obvious stopping-places like Laggan and Fort Augustus so you should be able to enjoy the scenery in peace. Certainly, there should be no traffic, as the nearest road is 2km away behind the trees.

From Kytra, the route continues along the towpath, the water looking less and less like a canal. It widens out into a basin, more akin to a small lochan than a navigational channel. The inlet bites into the land behind Kytra Loch, making it look as if the buildings are actually situated on an island. You will feel as if you are walking on an island too as the river on the left approaches the towpath again.

The first sign of Fort Augustus comes not with houses or cars but with golfers. Fort Augustus golf course lies on

The locks at Fort Augustus

the opposite bank of the canal, just before the towpath starts its gradual descent into the town; it nestles at the bottom of a hill and cannot be seen until you are almost upon it. The golf course is fringed by an avenue of tall Caledonian pines, standing like sentries guarding the approach to the town. Just as you have given up hope of ever reaching it, the towpath dips downwards and the canal falls away through the five locks which take it 12m down to the level of Loch Ness. From here the water on that most famous of lochs shines through a gap in the trees ahead.

The locks at Fort Augustus are likely to be the liveliest on the route. Lying halfway along the Great Glen – and marking the mid-point of your walk – the town is a popular mooring place for boats, as well as a favourite spot for tourists coming by road and on foot. The bustle of Fort Augustus may come as a bit of a shock after the days spent strolling undisturbed through forest and glen, when the only hint of commerce you will have encountered is a public bar on a boat. But you may also be grateful for the chance to replenish your supplies from the town's shops.

The highest of the five lock-gates offers a good vantage-point to watch all the activity. Building them was a major engineering feat. The poet Robert Southey describes a stage during their construction in 1820: 'Went before breakfast to look at the locks, five together. Such an extent of masonry upon such a scale, I had never before beheld, each of these locks being 180ft in length. It was a most impressive and remarkable scene. Men, horses and machines at work, digging, walling and puddling going on, men wheeling barrows, horses drawing stones along the railways.'

The locks are far deeper than they look. They were

exposed to the public gaze once again in 1996 when this section of the canal was drained to refurbish the sills on the gates as some of them had started to leak. Empty of water, the locks looked more like yawning chasms than the placid pools of normal operation.

The top lock is also a good place to get your bearings. Straight ahead of you, the canal flows into Loch Ness while to the right lies Fort Augustus Abbey and the remains of the old fort. To the left, hidden now behind the houses, the River Oich winds under the Inverness road to join Loch Ness. Just beside that bridge is the tourist information office.

Fort Augustus is well served with tourist facilities, from the basic room and breakfast on offer at the abbey to the plush rooms in the town's many hotels. In between, there is a range of bed and breakfasts, while those with tents can use the campsite a little way along the main road, heading back towards Fort William. There is plenty to occupy anyone wishing to celebrate

The River Oich where it enters Loch Ness

121

having reached the halfway point with a day at leisure. A museum of clan life is at the other side of the swing bridge. The museum in the abbey offers an interesting run through the history of northern Scotland, Loch Ness, the fort and the Benedictine monks who now occupy it.

Like Fort William, the town of Fort Augustus took its name from the military stronghold built here in 1742 and called in honour of Prince William Augustus who, as the Duke of Cumberland, was to become one of its most hated occupiers. Until then, the town was known as Kilcumein, its name derived from the church of Cumein, who was one of the disciples of St Columba. The monks were given the land of the abandoned fort by Lord Lovat in 1876, who had bought it from the government. Two years later, they opened a boarding school for boys which they ran until 1993 when education reforms and falling attendances made it uneconomic. Now, they aim to support themselves through tourist projects like the museum, a café and restaurant and boat trips. Even if you do not wish to take up any of these services, it is pleasant to walk around the grounds and admire the building, which is still impressive despite modern additions. To really appreciate the scale of the building, you need to climb a little way out of Fort Augustus – the approach to Meall a' Cholumain, a suggested excursion from here described at the end of the chapter, offers a good vantage-point.

A stroll to the top of the Meall a' Cholumain will not only give you a fantastic view of the route of the Great Glen Way, but will also allow you to say you have walked on the highest man-made road in Britain – the Corrieyairack Pass.

Fort Augustus is also a good place to savour the views

The abbey at Fort Augustus

of Loch Ness and get a taste of what lies ahead on the next two sections. The best viewpoint lies beyond the abbey at the loch's southernmost tip. Walk behind the abbey and across the Bridge of Tarff on the road towards Foyers until you reach the point where the loch shore starts to turn northwards once again. From here, on a clear day, you can see almost all the way along it, making this a far better place to appreciate its 36km (22-mile) length than the traditional viewpoint at the end of the canal. Even on a clear day, the erosion of the banks gives a hint of the power of the loch; when the skies are black and the wind is sweeping down the water, it seems a wild and isolated place.

Fort Augustus

Of the Great Glen's three main forts, Fort Augustus was the most strategically important. Positioned in the middle of the Glen, at the key crossroads for crofters and clansmen travelling south from the northern Highlands and islands, it was perfectly placed to serve the government's aim of 'checking some clans in the region who were unfavourable to the House of Hanover'.

Strategic position is not everything, however. Situated at the head of Loch Ness and surrounded by hills, the fort was all too vulnerable to surprise attack by the very clans it was supposed to subdue. General Wade, who was responsible for building the fort as well as the roads through the Glen, was always dubious about its location. In his report on the Highlands, he wrote: 'Two of them [the forts] are not built in as proper situations as they might have been.' And, in his first report to King George I in 1724, he wrote: 'It is to be wished that during the reign of Your Majesty and your successors, no insurrection may ever happen to experience whether the barracks will answer the end proposed.'

Wade did his best. Instead of using the existing barracks (part of the ramparts of which can still be seen in the grounds of the Lovat Hotel in the south-west of the town) he decided to build a new fort, an altogether more impressive building with more modern defences including angled bastions for artillery. Labourers were paid 7d a day (3p) for their efforts and the fort was eventually completed in 1742. The result looked impressive enough but even the first inhabitants were nervous. The garrison was isolated in the centre of the Glen and surrounded by hostile clans, making them extremely vulnerable to attack.

They did not have to wait long. Just three years after it was completed, the fort was blockaded by men from Clan Fraser; it took more than 600 troops to fight off the threat. The relief was short-lived, however. Three months later, Brigadier Stapleton and 300 Irish pickets, sent by Bonnie Prince Charlie to renew the blockade, quickly took control of the old fort. They then laid siege to the newly built garrison from trenches dug in a nearby hill, known as Battery Rock. Their luck was in; ten days after the siege began, a well-aimed shell hit the fort's gunpowder stores, with explosive results. The king's men had no choice but to surrender and the Jacobites quickly took control, taking the garrison's occupants as prisoners-of-war. That victory was, alas, rapidly followed by defeat at Culloden and the Jacobites fled. On 23 May 1746, William, Duke of Cumberland, marched from Inverness to take control of the fort. Thus began one of the bloodiest interludes in Scottish history as the troops butchered their way across the countryside, leaving smouldering houses and dying villagers in their wake. The brutal campaign earned the Duke the nickname Butcher Cumberland and the enduring bitterness of the Scots. Even to this day, the savagery of the oppression after Culloden is remembered in their choice of flowers; Sweet William, named in honour of the Duke – but called Bloody Willie in Scotland – is seldom planted here.

The Duke's passions were inflamed by what he found when he reached the fort. The Jacobites, determined not to surrender lightly, had dismantled as much of the fort as they could, forcing William and his men to camp in nearby fields – still known locally as Camp Fields. When they eventually returned to the garrison, they found the bodies of 11 English soldiers. The men were probably killed during the battle for control of the fort, but it was enough to rouse English tempers.

The Duke had taken nine regiments with him from Inverness and they were sent into the glens of north and west Scotland, burning all they found in their path.

When it was reported that Bonnie Prince Charlie had been sighted on the mainland, Cumberland sent 1,500 men to scour the west coast for the fugitive hero. No trace was found (the Prince was at the time hiding in a cave in Glenmoriston) but the local people suffered as the soldiers searched. So too did the English troops. Dom Odo Blundell, a monk who wrote an engaging history of Kilcumein and Fort Augustus, published by the abbey in 1914, records that the men returned from the hills 'fatigued and almost naked', but empty-handed. Shortly afterwards, Cumberland himself departed, expressing disappointment that his bloody campaign had not yielded better results. 'I am sorry to leave this country in the condition it is in; for all the good that we have done has been a little blood-letting, which has only weakened the madness, but not at all cured; and I tremble for fear that this vile spot may still be the ruin of this island and of our family.'

Some good did come out of Cumberland's bloody campaign, but in an unexpected way. The Ordnance Survey map was born in Fort Augustus as a way of helping the English soldiers track down the Scots in the surrounding countryside. At the time of the '45 rebellion, there were no reliable maps, which proved a serious drawback to Cumberland's campaigns. To remedy the position, a special detachment of infantry spent eight years from 1747 surveying the local area.

The driving force behind the maps was William Roy, a young engineer from Carluke in Lanarkshire. He was largely responsible for the creation of the first map, which is now in the British Museum, with a scale of 1,000 yards to an inch. It is an impressive piece of work, but Roy was a perfectionist: 'Although this work, which is still in manuscript, and in an unfinished state, possessed considerable merit, and perfectly answered the purpose for which it was originally intended; yet having been carried out with instruments of the common, or even inferior kind, and the sum allowed for it being inadequate to the execution of so great a design in the best manner, it is rather to be considered as a magnificent military sketch, than a very accurate map of the country,' he wrote.

That first map was never printed, although Roy did reduce it in size and reproduce it in one of his own books. It did, however, get him hooked on map-making: he took every opportunity to advocate the establishment of a national survey and he became surveyor-general of coasts and engineer for military surveys in Britain. Ordnance Survey was founded in 1791, a year after his death, a tribute to his tireless campaign.

As the rebellion fizzled out, the number of English troops stationed at the fort gradually dwindled. Eventually, in 1867, the government recognised that Fort Augustus was never going to be of strategic importance and the garrison was dismantled. Later that year it was sold to Lord Lovat, from whose family the lands were seized in the first place, for £5,000. Nine years later, Simon Fraser, Lord Lovat, gave it to some Scottish and English monks who had returned from Germany and wanted to form a monastery, and the abbey was built at a cost of some £120,000. The peppercorn rent he set then remains the charge today.

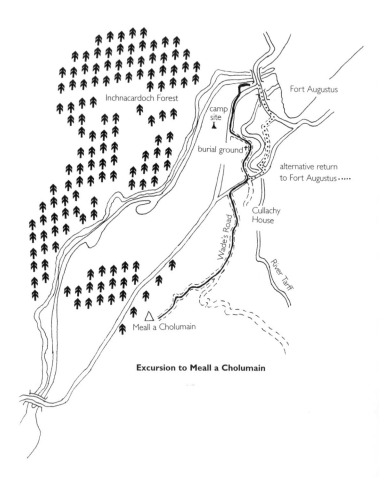

Inchnacardoch Forest

Fort Augustus

camp site

burial ground

alternative return to Fort Augustus .....

Wade's Road

Cullachy House

River Tarff

Meall a Cholumain

Excursion to Meall a Cholumain

Excursion 2
Meall a' Cholumain

Meall a' Cholumain is the perfect excursion for those who want to linger a while longer around Loch Ness and Fort Augustus. It is an easy stroll, taking perhaps three hours there and back, yet it gives good views along the Great Glen in both directions. What better way is there to celebrate reaching the halfway point of the route than by measuring progress so far and enjoying a preview of what's to come?

It also gives a chance to follow part of the Corrieyairack Pass, the highest and one of the most spectacular roads in Britain, and the most famous of the 250-mile network of roads throughout the Highlands whose building was supervised by General Wade between 1725 and 1732.

You will have noticed Meall a' Cholumain as you walked along the canal path from Aberchalder swing bridge to Fort Augustus. It is the rounded hill on the east side of the canal, identifiable by the television mast on its top. Begin at the canal bridge in Fort Augustus and head west along the towpath, this time on the south-eastern side. Turn left along Lovat Terrace then through the small alley between the bank and the row of alms-houses. The alley joins the main A82 road next to the town's police station. Turn right along the main road, heading away from Fort Augustus, past the green-painted Gondolier restaurant (named after the most famous of the pleasure steamers which used to ply Loch Ness).

At the Fort Augustus caravan and camping park, cross the road and follow the sign pointing to Kilcumein burial ground. The lane follows the tree-lined banks of the River Tarff then turns right away from the water towards the cemetery. Set on a hill and with the customary yew trees planted to ward off evil spirits, Kilcumein is well worth a visit. Look out for the grave of John Anderson, the carpenter who was the subject of the Robert Burns poem, 'John Anderson my Jo'. Also on a literary theme is a plaque commemorating the Gaelic poet Gilleasbuig Macdhomhnaill (Archibald MacDonald), who died *en route* to Inverness where he intended to publish his poems. The graveyard is also a sad memorial to the First World War. A number of gravestones commemorate the soldiers who died from the effects of gas, trench disease and war wounds in the period after the war ended, while being nursed at a sanatorium on the south shore of Loch Ness.

The route continues around the east wall of the cemetery and through the fields to join a minor road just opposite the entrance to Calachy Farm. Turn right along the road and continue past the grounds of Culachy House, with its impressive stands of beech, oak and sycamore trees, to a gate on the left with a sign on the metal railings identifying it as the start of General Wade's military road to Laggan over the Corrieyairack Pass.

The first few yards of the road are badly eroded, partly from the pounding of off-the-road vehicles whose drivers like to take advantage of the fact that the road remains a right of way, despite being a scheduled ancient monument. The gates and warnings about the penalties for damaging the road are an attempt to deter four-wheel drivers from continuing to use the road. After the first 100m, however, the road is in remarkably good

The start of the Corrieyairack Pass is now badly eroded

condition given that it was built more than 200 years ago and, with its summit at an exposed 752m (2,507ft), is constantly battered by snow, ice, wind and rain.

Its excellent condition is a testament to the skills of the 500 soldiers who built it during the summer of 1731 'for the better communication of His Majesty's troops'. They celebrated the completion of the 45km (28-mile) pass with a barbecue, with delicacies such as roast ox. Most now regard it as the high point – figuratively as well as literally – of General Wade's road-building career, although he himself was proudest of his bridges, particularly the rather ornate affair which crossed the Tay at Aberfeldy.

Wade's road-building accomplishments earned him the accolade of a verse, sung to the tune of the National Anthem, from a grateful Hanoverian poet. The reason for the roads' construction is clear from the words of the poem:

> *Lord, grant that Marshal Wade*
> *May, by thy mighty aid*
> *Victory bring*
> *May he sedition crush*
> *And like a torrent rush*
> *Rebellious Scotch to crush*
> *God save the king.*

Wade was sent to Scotland in 1724 after Lord Lovat wrote to King George I complaining that the Highlands were 'very mountainous and almost inaccessible to any but the inhabitants thereof' and were 'much less civilised than any other parts of Scotland'. Wade's brief was to 'inspect the situation of the Highlanders, their manners, customs and the state of the country in regard to the depredations said to be committed in that part of His Majesty's dominions'. His findings were alarming; in a report to George I he wrote that there were 10,000 loyal supporters of the king – and 12,000 more who would support a rebellion. 'The Highlands of Scotland are still more impractical from the want of roads and bridges,' he added, and recommended that the defences of the forts be bolstered and connected by roads through the Great Glen.

Before his road-building programme started, there were no roads in Scotland beyond Crieff and Dunkeld and travel was only possible on horseback, over rough tracks, In his *Letters from a Gentleman in the North of Scotland*, Edmund Burt commented: 'No stranger, or even a native unacquainted with the way, can venture among these hills without a conductor. The old ways consisted chiefly of stony moors, rugged, rapid fords, declivities of hills, entangling woods and giddy precipices.'

Sixty years later, the Highlands of Scotland had been transformed by the building of more than 1,760km (1,100 miles) of roads and 938 bridges. Wade himself was responsible for only 400km (250 miles) of road and 40 bridges – the work was continued by his assistant, Major William Caulfield, who led the programme between 1740 and 1767. But it is with Wade that Scotland's road-building is mainly associated. He was certainly a colourful character. Born in 1673, he joined the army in 1690 staying long enough to fight for the Duke of Cumberland at Culloden at the ripe old age of 72. He died three years later, leaving a substantial fortune, and was honoured for his loyalty to the crown with burial in Westminster Abbey.

He was clearly proud of his road-building efforts. On completion of the road between Fort Augustus and Fort William he wrote: 'The great road of communication is so far advanced that I travelled to Fort William in my coach-and-six to the great wonder of the country people, who had never seen such a machine in these parts before.' Others agreed. Burt admired the transformation wrought by Wade: 'The roads on these moors are now as smooth as Constitution Hill,' he wrote.

Wade may have engineered the road, but the route across the Corrieyairack had been in use for years. It was the most direct route from the north-western Highlands and islands for drovers taking their cattle to trysts at Crieff and Falkirk, while Montrose and his army of mountaineers followed its route on their march to Fort William to spring their surprise on Campbell's men camped at Inverlochy Castle.

Wade's aim was to link the army bases at Fort Augustus and Ruthven at the other end of the pass, but it was Bonnie Prince Charlie's men who came closest to triumphing from its use. After raising his standard at Glenfinnan, the Prince led his men across the pass, hoping to meet the troops of General Sir John Cope, the commander of the government forces. From the summit of the pass, he intended to bombard Cope's men as they struggled up the 18 steep zigzags which lie just below the summit. Cope's army, Charlie reckoned, would be ill-suited to such hostile terrain, so his clansmen, whose lives had been spent on hills and passes such as these, would be guaranteed victory.

Cope was not to be so easily tricked. Anticipating Charlie's tactics, he sidestepped to Ruthven barracks instead of tackling the pass, allowing the Prince to march unopposed to Perth. While Cope was court-martialled for dereliction of duty, he was pardoned when it became clear that confronting the Jacobites on the pass would have meant certain defeat.

For a hundred years, the Corrieyairack Pass was the highest maintained public road in Britain, but it gradually fell out of use during the 19th century. It is not hard to appreciate why. Wade described it as 'easy and practicable for wheeled carriages as any road in the country'. Others were less sure.

An early traveller called Skrine complained that it was an 'inexpressibly arduous road . . . springing sometimes from point to point over alpine bridges and at other times pursuing narrow ridges of rock frightfully impending over tremendous precipices'. Another described it as impassable in depths of winter, adding that it was: 'particularly dangerous not only from deep snows concealing the unbeaten track of the road, but from whirlwinds and eddies that drive the snow into heaps'. Thomas Telford, whose own route to connect Fort Augustus and the Great Glen with the east central Highlands is followed by the modern A82, described the pass as 'so inconveniently steep as to be nearly unfit for the purposes of civil life'. Nevertheless, the 19km (12 miles) between here and Melgarve, on the descent from the pass, remain the longest surviving stretch of an original Wade road. Walking along it is an enjoyable way of experiencing a part of Scotland's history.

Go through the gate and begin the walk along the road, taking care on the more eroded areas. In the early summer the gorse which lines the path emits its familiar coconut smell, while the edges of the path are peppered with plants like yellow and purple saxifrage. The condition of the road quickly improves, leaving time to savour the views back towards Fort Augustus and Loch Ness – these get even better higher up. Ahead are the imposing ramparts of Culachy House. Just before it, a road branches off to the left, crossed a little way down by a pretty bridge.

Beyond the house, a gate bristling with warning signs aimed at deterring four-wheel-drive enthusiasts marks the transition from the more pastoral, wooded terrain which you have been walking through so far, into the open moorland of heather and peat which stretches all the way across the hills to Laggan on the other side. Technically, this area is known as the Corrieyairack forest but, like many Scottish 'forests', the description applies to areas where deer roam, rather than to woodlands. In the winter months, you may spot herds of deer coming down from the high tops in search of food.

The road climbs to a summit and passes under a line of electricity pylons. From here, you can see Wade's road stretching off into the distance as it climbs over the hills to Laggan. To the south, a wide rolling glen leads towards

The view westwards

Aberchalder. The path up to Meall a' Cholumain leaves the Corrieyairack here on a track which branches right. It climbs gradually but steadily up the hill, past the ruins of the old croft Knollbuck, with ever-widening views back across the hills. You may not be climbing to the summit of the Corrieyairack, but you will still be going high enough to notice a change in the temperature; even on a fine day, it is worth taking extra warm and water-proof clothes in case there is a wind on the top of the hill or to cope with a sudden change in the weather.

The climb to the television mast is quickly over. The top of the hill is broad and featureless, riven with peat hags and heather. But for such an inconsequential peak,

the view is spectacular. Savour first the north-eastern side, where the abbey can be seen at the tip of Loch Ness, its waters glittering silver as it winds its narrow way to Inverness.

The best view, however, is to the west. Walk on past the mast through the heather and peat for a little way for fine views back down the Great Glen to Fort William. Closest is the small Loch Oich, looking even more perfect from this angle; beyond it is the broader expanse of Loch Lochy. On a clear day, you can even see all the way to Loch Linnhe and the Atlantic beyond.

The beauty of the loch is offset by the glorious greens and russet-yellows of the hills around them: Ben Tee, Meall na Teanga, Sron a' Choire Ghairbh and the other hills of the Great Glen. Directly below is the route into Fort Augustus along the Caledonian Canal.

To return to Fort Augustus, retrace your steps past Knollbuck and back onto the Corrieyairack. Fort Augustus beckons ahead of you and, as you get closer, you can pick out the remains of the pier beyond the abbey which was built to take passengers from the railway onto the loch's steamboats.

For a different way to return to Fort Augustus, continue along the minor road beyond Culachy Farm instead of branching left to Kilcumein. The road dips down to a high, single-arched bridge across the River Tarff. Just beyond the bridge, a track branches left towards Ardachy Lodge. Take this track, then branch right to pass through pleasant woodlands and meadows on the way towards Fort Augustus.

The track joins the narrow road along the south side of Loch Ness. Turn left to return to Fort Augustus. The grounds of the abbey on the right are strewn with wild garlic, its pungent smell filling the air on a summer's day.

The road can be busy in the height of the tourist season and there is no pavement, but it is only a short walk back to the starting point at the canal bridge.

Fort Augustus to Invermoriston

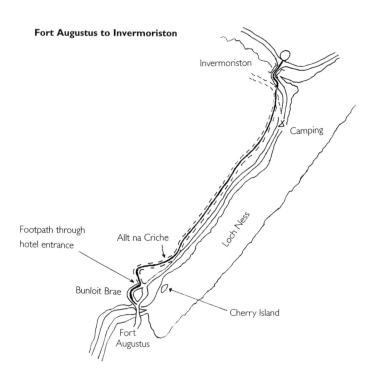

Invermoriston

Camping

Footpath through
hotel entrance

Allt na Criche

Loch Ness

Bunloit Brae

Cherry Island

Fort
Augustus

Section 6
Fort Augustus to Invermoriston

When you leave Fort Augustus you also leave the Caledonian Canal behind; the next time the Great Glen Way meets it is close to its end in Inverness. If you decide on the alternative route into Inverness described at the end of Section 8, you will join it again at its very end, where it empties into the Beauly Firth. The move away from the canal will be obvious from more than just the change in the scenery; so far, the climbing has been minimal as the Great Glen Way made use of towpaths and lochside tracks. From now on, however, it winds up and down the hills which swoop down to the loch shore, so there will be more to test your legs and lungs. More, but still not much: the climbs are generally gradual and even the steepest, which lie between Invermoriston and Inverness on the next sections of the route, are short. With 56km (35 miles) of the Way already completed, you should not be defeated by a few steep slopes.

What the route misses in canal vistas it more than makes up for in views of Loch Ness. The narrow fiord of the loch will dominate the scenery for most of the next three sections, its sparkling waters appearing suddenly from clearings in the trees as you proceed along the route. Loch Ness is a place for superlatives. It is not the longest loch in Britain nor the deepest, but on virtually every other count Loch Ness beats all-comers. Glaciers hollowed out the rock already weakened by the shifting of the fault to create a vast, deep basin; its lowest point is 229m (750ft) – deeper than the North Sea. It holds the

Leaving Fort Augustus

most water – three times as much as Loch Lomond and more than all the lakes and reservoirs of England and Wales put together. It takes water from eight rivers and 40 burns drawn from a 1,775 square km area, making it one of the largest freshwater systems in Europe. Only one river, the River Ness, flows out of it, so its level can rise very rapidly after heavy rain.

There is still some dispute about the origin of the name Ness. Some say it derives from Nyfus, an Irish hero whose fortress was at Dun Dearduil further along on the south side of the loch, while others say it means Loch of the Falls from the Gaelic word *es* (water), after the striking waterfalls above Foyers.

The depth of the loch means the water never freezes, and it stays at a consistent temperature: consistently cold. All but the most hardy of swimmers would baulk at dipping even a toe never mind their entire body into it on even the most tropical of days. There are some hardy swimmers around, however: one, Brenda Sherratt, swam its entire length in 1966, taking 18½ hours to do so. The depth and coldness of the water means it contains only a few species of fish, including pike, eels (sometimes pure white, if they have spent most of their time deep in the water), salmon and the rare Arctic char, which lives in only a few deep waters in Britain. There is also, of course, the world's most famous monster, Nessie. Be sure to keep your camera handy on the next two sections – a snatched picture of the monster's head could be worth a fortune!

You will have plenty of opportunity for monster-spotting on the way to Invermoriston. This section of the Way clings to the steep sides of Carn an Doire Mhoir, on a forestry track which winds above the loch's north-western shoreline. These dense but varied forest sections are interspersed with regular views of the loch and across to the hills of Glendoe and beyond on the opposite shore.

To begin, make your way to the carpark which lies next to the tourist information office on the road to Inverness. As you cross the bridge over the River Oich, look in both directions to see earlier versions of the river crossing. On the left are the ramparts of an old stone bridge; on the right is an old wooden trestle bridge, now dilapidated and closed to pedestrian and vehicle traffic.

Just after the carpark, Bannoich Brae climbs the hill to the left. Take that road, past the Brae Hotel with its splendid situation overlooking the town, and take the right fork at the village hall. Cross the small stone bridge that spans the Balantoul Burn and continue past a row of cottages on the right which were once alms-houses. The road dips again and curves gradually round to the right, until it rejoins the A82 a little way outside Fort Augustus.

The Way turns off to the left just before the A82, between the white stone gateposts which mark the side

Looking back to Fort Augustus

entrance of the drive to the Inchnacardoch Lodge Hotel. Leave the drive about 10m along it on a path which crosses the burn on the left and climbs up the tree-lined slope at the other side. This is a right of way into the forest which lies further up the hill. A number of small paths branch off in various directions as you climb the slope, but stick to the main track as it climbs steadily at first, then quite steeply, through birch trees and then magnificent pines. The climb is quickly over, ending at a wide forest track which runs along the side of the hill.

The regimented conifers in a new plantation on the left-hand side of the track are soon replaced by a more varied mixture of types and ages of tree and the walking

is pleasant, with excellent views back down to the town below. The pointed roof of the abbey peeps out through the trees in its grounds, while behind you the Great Glen stretches away towards Fort William.

Below you on the right you will soon see the small scrap of land which claims the distinction of being the only island on Loch Ness. It is man-made, however; the glacier scoured the floor of the Glen so thoroughly that no trace of land remained above the water level. Cherry Island, or Eilean Muireach, is in fact a crannog, the name given to these small Bronze Age dwellings which were often built on lochs across the Highlands. There are faint remains of another crannog in Loch Oich, while one on

Cherry Island, Loch Ness

Loch Lochy was reputedly still in use in the 16th century, when the chiefs of the Mackintosh clan built it to mount their raids on the lands of Lochaber.

The crannog on Loch Ness was known as Eilean Muireach, Murdoch's island, until Oliver Cromwell's

146

men renamed it the more pronounceable, if less accurate, Cherry Island. It was only identified as a crannog in 1908 when Dom Odo Blundell, a monk from Fort Augustus Abbey, borrowed diving gear from Caledonian Canal workers and discovered that it was man-made. Although nowadays it bristles with tall pine trees, the construction of crannogs resulted in the destruction of much of the natural forest which once covered the entire Great Glen. Crannogs were made from oak beams tied together to make a floor, which was then overlaid with rubble and topped with larger boulders to ensure the structure was strong enough to withstand the pressure of the water. The construction has proved durable, although a smaller crannog nearby, Eilean nan Con, possibly used to house dogs, was submerged by the building of the canal. The weir at Dochgarroch, built for the construction of the canal, raised the level of Loch Ness by two metres, totally submerging the smaller crannog and cutting the surface area of the remaining one to 18m by 14m. Before the weir was built it had been closer to 20m by 16m.

The purpose of crannogs is not completely clear. This one may have been a castle, accessible by a causeway from the shore. Or it may have been a hunting lodge, a theory supported by the presence of the smaller island for dogs nearby. There is evidence that it was occupied right up until the 15th century, and it would certainly have been a good place to ensure that the inhabitants were kept safe from the unwelcome attentions of local clans and other marauders.

On the shore to the right of the crannog you can see the jetty built so that trains could stop right next to ferries from Inverness. The Highland Railway's efforts to frustrate the service unfortunately proved all too successful. It is still possible to pick out faint traces of the track back to Fort Augustus.

The Way now becomes a pleasant stroll along a well-laid path, with frequent stunning views down to the loch. Small streams tumble down the hill to the water some 80m (260ft) below, the ferocity of their flow – and the drama of their waterfalls – depending on the time of year and extent of rainfall. Although this is clearly a commercial forest, it is not at all oppressive; the variety of trees – who would have guessed there could be so many types of evergeens? – and different ages make it a most attractive place. Nor are the trees planted densely enough to block out the views down to the loch.

The path drops down to Allt na Criche, where a carpark and forest walks have been created by Forest Enterprise. This was the point where the old drove road from the northern Highlands and from Skye and the Western Isles reached the Great Glen, continuing the long march south to the cattle markets in Falkirk and Stirling via the Corrieyairack Pass. The animals thus transported were black cattle, a breed of small cow, which are immortalised still in the word blackmail, though few who use the word, or its techniques, will realise it. Blackmail derives from the practice of clan chiefs demanding payments from crofters in an early version of the protection racket. Those who paid the tariff or 'blackmeal' were left undisturbed, while those who refused were liable to sudden attack from the clansmen and the loss of their black cattle.

Climb up from the carpark again through a magnificent stand of Douglas firs, planted more than 60 years ago. A clear-felled area gives a splendid viewpoint to contemplate the loch in both directions and is also a good place from which to pick out the distinctive shape of the Horseshoe Crags on the opposite shore of the loch. Part of the Easterness Forest, designated a site of special scientific interest, the forest on the crag is inaccessible to all but the most intrepid and dogged of wildlife enthusiasts. That inaccessibility means it is well preserved as one of the best examples of what Britain's ancient forests looked like. Birch is the dominant species, but it is interspersed with oak, ash, hazel and aspen, with Scots pine, holly and juniper taking over where the soil is thinner and less fertile. Under the trees is a profusion of native plants, from wild strawberry and blaeberry to wood sage and golden rod. Those who want to see it for themselves would be well advised to go by boat; getting to it on foot can be extremely dangerous.

The path winds slowly round to the left, gradually bringing Invermoriston into view up ahead. Just as you see the first signs of habitation, a clear path rises to meet the track from the right. Down here is Rubha Ban, the closest campsite to Invermoriston. Continue along the main track to where it divides in two. Both the higher and lower routes wind some distance round the side of Sron na Muic, dropping down to the River Moriston some way up Glen Moriston. That makes it a long walk back to the village of Invermoriston and it is best to avoid the unnecessary detour by heading straight down towards the road from here. The plans for an official Great Glen Way include a new path in this area. Until it is built, go through a gap in the wall near where the two paths diverge and head downhill towards the A82. The most direct and easiest route joins the A82 a little way outside Invermoriston. Take care when walking along the road until you reach a pavement just before the bridge.

Invermoriston is a tiny village, little more than a staging-post on the famous Road to the Isles which runs up Glen Moriston from here. Its most interesting feature is the old bridge, lying just to the left of the current bridge which carries the A82 across the river. Built by Thomas Telford, it is one of a thousand constructed between 1808 and 1819 to improve communications in the Highlands. This one was rather ill-fated, however, an early indication of the pitfalls of using private money for public projects. Started in 1805, its construction was dogged by delays and idle contractors. The private businessman who undertook the project agreed to finance it but, by the time it was finally completed in 1813, costs had soared to many times the original estimate, and the poor man had been made bankrupt. That bridge was damaged in the floods of 1951. The bridge which replaced it was built in 1954 and is a good spot from which to admire Telford's handiwork on the old one.

The great engineer built two other bridges across the River Moriston, one at Torgyle (which was washed away

The old bridge at Invermoriston

about ten years ago) and the other at Ceannacroc, near the inn where Dr Johnson and his friend James Boswell stayed during their Highland tour in 1773. Never a particular fan of the Scots or Scotland, Johnson described the people as poor, but gradually recovering from the effects of the '45 rebellion. He expressed great surprise that the keeper of the inn where he stayed (which is now a sheep pen) was educated and, to mark his approval, gave the man's daughter a book on arithmetic.

An earlier and rather more welcome visitor to Ceannacroc was Bonnie Prince Charlie, who hid in a cave in the area under the protection of the Seven Men of Glen Moriston on his flight after the Battle of Culloden. It was while he was a fugitive there that Roderick Mackenzie, an officer in his army, probably saved the Prince's life. Trying to escape from the pursuing English, he was hit by a Redcoat's musket ball just by the spot where he knew the Prince was hiding. As he fell, Mackenzie cried out: 'You have killed your prince!' Red-haired and bearing a passing physical resemblance to Charlie, Mackenzie's dying words persuaded the enemy that they had assassinated the Young Pretender. His head was triumphantly transported to the Duke of Cumberland at Fort Augustus by soldiers eager to share in the £30,000 reward offered for the Prince's capture. The deception was eventually uncovered – but not before the Prince had been given time to make his escape. A cairn marking the site of Mackenzie's death lies near Ceannacroc in Glen Moriston.

A rather more bizarre memorial, and a site of pilgrimage, lies closer to Invermoriston in the Glen: Finlay Munro's footsteps. According to local legend, they appeared in 1827 as the preacher Finlay attempted to demonstrate the power of the Lord to doubters.

The river which the two bridges span once had impressive waterfalls but nowadays the waterflow is controlled by the Dundreggan dam, which feeds the underground power station of the same name further up Glen Moriston, and it is rare to see the falls in full flow.

Timber from Glen Moriston has long been used in industry. In 1249, ships for the crusades were built using pine and oak from forests in the glen and its pine trees were also called upon for the construction of the Caledonian Canal. The logs were floated down the river to the loch and taken to the canal workings by boat. Birch from the glen was used to make barrels for fishermen from the east coast – the building on the north side of the bridge once housed the smithy which made the barrels. Timber remains a key industry for the Glen Moriston area today, with much of the land round about owned by the Forestry Commission.

The area around Invermoriston is one of the few flat sections of the Loch Ness shoreline. The steepness of the banks, together with the fierceness of the waves when the wind is up, means that aquatic plants are rare and confined to a few areas like this and around Drumna-drochit. It is an excellent place for spotting some of the wildlife the loch attracts, including birds like the reed bunting, sedge warbler and Arctic tern, which can sometimes be seen dive-bombing intruders who stray too close to its nest. Heron are common and you may even see a kingfisher or spot a white-chested dipper using its strong claws as anchors to 'walk' along the loch bed in search of larvae.

One of the animals you are unlikely to see is the Urquhart puma. One of these big cats was captured in a trap on the shore of Loch Ness near here and moved to

Kincraig wildlife park, where she died of old age in 1985. Her body was stuffed and can now be seen in Inverness Museum.

Invermoriston has a hotel, a pub and a village store. A number of houses around the village also offer bed and breakfast in season. A little way along the loch shore at Alltsigh, accessible from further along the route of the Great Glen Way, is a youth hostel.

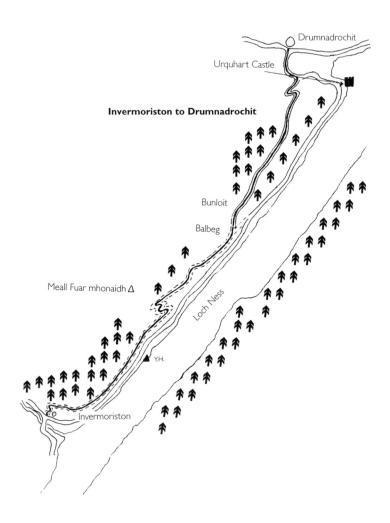

Invermoriston to Drumnadrochit

Drumnadrochit

Urquhart Castle

Bunloit

Balbeg

Loch Ness

Meall Fuar mhonaidh △

Y.H.

Invermoriston

Section 7
Invermoriston to Drumnadrochit

This section of the Great Glen Way provides the most testing ascent so far. The route to Drumnadrochit starts with a long climb out of Invermoriston round the lower slopes of Carn Mor. There is then a gradual descent to the loch shore again at Alltsigh, followed by another climb up the slopes of Creag Dhearg. It's not worth looking for alternative routes as none of the climbs is long or particularly arduous, just enough to get the heart working properly and the leg muscles singing.

The first climb starts almost immediately. From the Invermoriston Arms Hotel, walk a short way along the road through Glen Moriston then turn right up the steep hill which winds up behind the hotel heading for Achnaconeran. The road zigzags steeply through a pretty, mixed forest, with good views back down towards the bay around the mouth of the River Moriston.

The climbing ends just after the natural forest gives way to the denser coniferous trees which mark a commercial plantation. Here, the Way turns off the main road onto a forest track to the right through thickly planted but attractive trees, and winds its way round the lower slopes of Carn Mor. A short distance along the path, the trees thin out and your climbing effort is rewarded with a wonderful view down the loch, now nestling some 200m (650ft) below you in the Glen. A new plantation of trees on the left of the path is guarded by a densely packed 'hedge' of small trees. At the edge of the plantation, a gate marks the end of the forest and the start of open countryside, where views on all sides open up. As well as the now familiar loch shore, there are splendid views up towards the summit of Carn Mor, largely hidden from view by the cliffs of Sgor Gaoithe. These are steep enough to look unclimbable, but that has not deterred a few trees from planting their roots in the rocky crags.

The forest track continues around the flanks of the steep hill then seems to come to a dead end. Just before the end, the Way turns downhill on a steeply zigzagging path on the right, its start marked by two posts, which descends towards the loch shore once again. Before heading downhill, it is worth climbing a few extra steps to the viewpoint a couple of metres along the track. There, a small wooden bench provides a resting place to enjoy the views back along the water towards Fort Augustus. That end of the loch will shortly be concealed behind the steep crags ahead of you. You can see back to the end of the last section where the Way dropped into Invermoriston from the forestry path and, on a clear day, you may even be able to pick out the spires of the abbey, as well as the TV mast on the top of Meall a' Cholumain above Fort Augustus.

The steep but short descent ends at another forest track which continues along the side of Creag nan Eun. This is one of the best parts of the Great Glen Way for plant-spotting; as well as large clumps of harebells and primroses in the late spring, you may also be able to spot the insect-eating butterwort (with its tell-tale star-shaped leaves), dog violet, milkwort and lousewort lining the paths; further into the forest, small clumps of mountain azalea are interspersed with the more familiar heather, gorse and blaeberry bushes. Such a variety of plants and shrubs attracts insects and birds. The tap-tap of woodpeckers can often be heard among the trees, while the distinctive sound of the cuckoo echoes across the glen in spring. Smaller birds like the pipit, whinchat and willow warbler dart from the ground as you pass, and you may see a crossbill determinedly bashing a swollen pine-cone in its search for seeds. Occasionally, high above you, you might spot the predatory circling of one of the area's birds of prey, such as the buzzard, sparrow-hawk or golden eagle.

The route rises and falls gently as it winds its way along the sides of the loch. On the left-hand side, a small cave is cut into the steep bank, making an ideal spot to picnic in bad weather. Looking across the loch towards Creag Mhor and the other steep hills on the banks of the loch, it is easy to appreciate why forestry is such an important industry in this area. So intense was the scarring by the glaciers that the slopes left behind when the ice moved on are too precipitous to support anything but the most tenacious of plants. Indeed, as you can see, some of the slopes are even too steep for the Forestry Commission to use for plantations.

Above you loom the steep rocky slopes of Meall na Sroine. The path climbs once more through heather, bracken and gorse, enlivened in the early summer by splashes of colour from the encroaching rhododendron and in late summer by the purple glow of heather. The track drops gradually towards the level of the loch at Alltsigh, crossing the Allt Saigh river on a modern concrete bridge. If you look carefully through the trees on the right, you can make out the remains of a hump-backed bridge which was the old packhorse route across the river before the A82 road was built. Just beyond the bridge, a track turns off to the right and heads down to the road and the Loch Ness youth hostel.

157

The old bridge near Alltsigh

The Way continues up the hill through mature forest, climbing steadily once again. A succession of burns tumble down the steep slopes towards the loch, some of which are steep enough to make spectacular waterfalls. As the slope of the path eases, the trees give way to an area of clear-felling, allowing good views across the loch to the buildings of Foyers on the other side of the loch. The pipes, factories and large warehouses are an incongruous sight amid the rural landscape. This is Britain's first major commercial hydro-electric power station (which is still in operation today, albeit with some modern modifications) and the remains of the aluminium smelter (again the first to be built in Britain, but now closed).

The smelter opened in 1895 and was operated by British Aluminium, who also built the one seen at the start of the route in Fort William. Even the Nazis had heard of its importance: it was bombed in February 1941 by a lone Heinkel III, which dropped two 500-pound bombs on it. One worker was killed, but the damage to the factory was minimal. Production of aluminium continued here until 1967, when the smelter was deemed no longer viable and closed.

The power station was sold to the Hydro-Electric Board, now Scottish Hydro, who converted it to a pump storage scheme. Water feeds into the station from Loch Mhor behind the hills, drains into Loch Ness at the rate of 200 tonnes of water a second and is then pumped back up to Loch Mhor again. Even at that speed, it would take 152 days to empty the loch. The 247-tonne transformer at the power station was transported from Inverness by boat, and is the largest load ever to have used the Caledonian Canal.

Just beyond here, the forest track splits in two. One branch heads on towards the trees but the Way lies uphill, on a seemingly endless series of zigzags which take you to the upper edge of the forest. The second climb of this section may be longer but it is more gentle than the first. Fix your eyes on the highest of the few solitary

Caledonian pines which dot the empty landscape above; the track does not level out until it has passed above that one. Birds of prey often perch in these lonesome pines, swooping off to higher ground as you approach.

The long zigzags eventually end just as a track joins the Way from the left. You have reached the highest point on the Great Glen Way so far – about 300m (almost 1,000ft) above the level of the loch. You are rewarded with good views back through the Great Glen and to the south-east. Indeed, you have now climbed high enough to see over the first row of hills on the east side of the loch and on into the massed ranks of the Monadhliath mountains which lie beyond. On a clear day, it is even possible to pick out Braeriach, Ben Macdui and other peaks of the Cairngorms which lie in the distance behind Foyers.

The Way continues along the path right, heading into the forest once more. The track is wide and clear and the cushion of pine-needles will be welcome after the long climb. In late spring the path is strewn with wild primroses, adding a flash of brightness against the green of the trees, while azalea and heather ensure the colour continues through the summer months. Blaeberries provide a refreshing fruit snack in the late summer, and attract birds. Note also the huge ant-hills which line the edges of the forest – choose a place to stop and rest with care!

The high forest track comes to a large gate, then carries on beyond it on a specially created link path for the Great Glen Way and cycle route to join another forest track in the woods ahead of you. Already the path is being colonised by mountain flowers like saxifrage, milkwort and mixed grasses, and it will soon look as natural a part of the hillside as the gorse and bracken

The track branches left to Bunloit

which surround it. Take care as you walk along, however, as it is narrow in places and the ground slopes steeply down towards the loch below.

At the end of the link path, rejoin the forest track for a very short distance. After 50m, a path climbs up to the left along the edge of an ancient oak forest surrounded by a high wire fence. Take this path through a recently erected kissing gate (designed to keep both cyclists and deer out) and head round the edge of the forest towards the small settlement of Grotaig. At the eastern edge of the forest, their location well hidden behind the oak trees, lie the remnants of another of the Great Glen's old forts, Dun Scriben.

A small white cottage with a red corrugated roof is the first sign of habitation, but it is soon joined by a number of crofts and outbuildings (one of which now houses a small pottery shop) which mark the start of the tarmac road you will follow down to Drumnadrochit. Above Grotaig is the rounded hump of Meall Fuar-mhonaidh, which will be instantly recognisable to those who climbed Sron a' Choire Ghairbh from Laggan. One of the highest hills at this end of the Glen, its distinctive mound will remain a feature of the landscape until the Way climbs over to Achpopuli to begin the final descent into Inverness. The energetic can take a detour up this hill by following the path signposted just behind the last of the farm buildings.

This was the site of an incident in the long-running feud between the Mackenzies of Ross and the Glengarry MacDonnells in the 17th century. The MacDonnells burnt the church of Cill a Chrioso, in which members of the Mackenzie clan were worshipping. Allan MacRonnaill, leader of the aggressors, fled up the braes of Meall Fuar-mhonaidh, and across a gorge of the Allt Suidhe, one of the burns which flow down its flanks. In hot pursuit was one of the Mackenzies, whose misfortune continued as he failed in his attempt to leap across the burn, just saving himself by clutching at an overhanging birch branch. MacRonnaill showed no mercy this time either. Turning to the stranded Mackenzie, he said: 'I have left much behind me with you today. Take that also.' With those words, he cut the branch and the hapless Mackenzie plunged to his death in the gorge below.

Cross a small wooden bridge which spans the Grotaig Burn and head north-east along the quiet road which meanders up and down through open countryside, now pasture, now peat and heather bogland. While a large part of the route so far has been dominated by views south-east across the Glen, most of the rest of the Way from here to Inverness gives vast panoramas to the north-west too. Already, you will be able to see the distant hills surrounding Loch Affric and Loch Monar away in the

On the way to Bunloit

163

west; the snow which clings to the tops of the hills off in the distance well into the early summer months is an indication of their impressive height.

The road passes the farm buildings of Balbeg, where the remains of houses and an old sheep pen hint that this moorland was once rather more densely populated than it is today. Next is the small hamlet of Bunloit and a variety of scattered crofts and cottages, which are joined by the familiar wooden chalets of the traditional Scottish holiday park.

The open moorland eventually gives way to forest, with some particularly fine examples of Scots pine. A short way through the woods, the road starts to descend, then dips steeply down towards Lewiston. As it does so, you will get your first sight of the scattered buildings of Drumnadrochit, the end-point of this section. Take care on the steep bends of the hills and listen out for traffic.

The road levels out again just as it approaches the hamlet of Lewiston and joins the main A82 road. Cross it before the bridge where there is a path on the grass verge, which soon becomes pavement running all the way round to Drumnadrochit. The villages of Lewiston and Drumnadrochit now merge into each other, but once they were separate. Lewiston was a planned town, created and built by local landowner Sir James Grant who called it after his son Lewis. It has a supermarket, a number of guest-houses and places offering bed and breakfast. More B&B accommodation lies a little further along the road in Drumnadrochit, which also has a post office with a small shop attached, a bank and a few hotels.

Walkers who decide to stay here for the night have a range of attractions to visit. Not to be missed, whether

Urquhart Castle

you are staying or travelling straight on, is Urquhart Castle, once Scotland's largest and still one of its most scenic. Perched on a promontory overlooking Loch Ness at the end of Urquhart Bay, the castle's excellent defensive position has long been recognised and there is evidence of strongholds on the site going back as far as the Bronze Age, when there was a fort on the promontory.

A royal castle, Urquhart played a major role in most parts of Scottish history, including the Wars of Independence, the conflicts between the kings of

Scotland and the Lords of the Isles and, of course, the Jacobite rebellion. It was constantly sacked, taken by the enemy, recaptured by the Scots, burnt down and rebuilt. The main buildings of the castle as it stands date from the 14th century, although parts of the citadel go back a hundred years before that. On the land side, its ramparts were defended by a huge dry ditch, which was crossed by a stone causeway and a wooden drawbridge. The gatehouse was blown up, probably by royal troops intent on keeping Jacobites out following William of Orange's accession to the throne.

William Wallace, the legendary Scottish hero, seized it from English hands as he made his triumphal sweep across Scotland at the end of the 13th century. The Scots were soon displaced by the English again, however; soldiers of Edward I captured it in 1303 after a long siege designed to starve the occupants into submission. During the siege, Sir Alexander Forbes smuggled his pregnant wife out of the castle by disguising her as a peasant. She fled to Ireland, where her son was born, but not before she had stood on the outcrop known as Eagle Rock and witnessed her husband launch a doomed attempt to break out of the siege. Her son eventually returned to Scotland, where he was rewarded by the gift of substantial land from another occupant of the castle, Robert the Bruce.

One of the worst periods of the castle's history was not in battle, however, but during the time it was occupied by Buchan, son of the Scottish king, Robert II. He acquired it in 1390 and used his power to terrorise the local countryside and refused to pay his dues. He married the widowed Countess of Ross, promptly abusing her and being unfaithful. He even stooped to sacking churches, for which he was excommunicated, and in a real fit of temper burnt the town of Forres in north-east Scotland and sacked the cathedrals of Elgin and Moray. He was eventually brought to book by the Church, which forced him to abject penance for his sins.

The castle is not Drumnadrochit's only attraction. Further along the loch shore, beyond Urquhart Castle, is the memorial to John Cobb's fatal attempt to beat the world water speed record on Loch Ness in 1936, and there are older monuments aplenty in the area. Drumnadrochit is surrounded by ancient forts. Apart from Dun Scriben which the Way passed above Grotaig, there is also a vitrified fort, Craig Mony, on a hill high above the town; a visit to it takes you through one of the finest stands of Scots pine in the Great Glen. The trees in Urquhart Bay itself, known locally as the Cover, are also part of an ancient woodland. At the northern end of the bay, a small religious house belonging to the Knights of the Temple once stood. Although it has now been demolished, the area is still known as the Temple, and a landing point on the bay is called Temple Pier. Further up Glen Urquhart is Corrimony chambered cairn, surrounded by slabs and standing stones.

For those with a more literary interest, it is worth visiting Dhivach Lodge, perched on a hill high above the loch above the spectacular 100ft Dhivach Falls, which in its time has played host to writers and actors such as J.M. Barrie, creator of Peter Pan, Anthony Trollope and Sir John Gielgud. A trip up to see the falls and lodge is a pleasant walk – the best way is to take the road which climbs south from Lewiston on the west side of the bridge across the River Coiltie. The falls look less spectacular from the top, where the viewpoint is located,

THE GREAT GLEN WAY

than they would from the bottom; access to that area, however, is unfortunately impossible.

And then, of course, there is the Loch Ness Monster.

The Loch Ness Monster

It is a little surprising that of the 1,200-odd labourers who struggled with the construction of the Caledonian Canal at either end of Loch Ness, the thousands of passengers who plied its waters on steamboats for more than a hundred years, not to mention all those involved in digging its south-eastern banks to build the power station at Foyers or blasting the rocks to construct the A82 on its other side, not one of them ever mentioned seeing anything resembling a monster. Yet, since 1933, the words 'Loch Ness' and 'Monster' have been inextricably linked, and reports of sightings of Nessie as common as the scientific theories which 'prove' it really could exist.

It all started quietly enough. On 3 May 1933, the *Inverness Courier* reported 'A Strange Spectacle on Loch Ness'. A year later, Harley Street gynaecologist R.K. Wilson published *that* photograph in the *Daily Mail,* the fuzzy black-and-white shot which generations of monster-hunters believe is the perfect shot of Nessie posing for the camera. Sceptics, on the other hand, dismiss it as no more mysterious than the tail of a diving otter. Since then, Nessie has become an institution. Sightings are reported regularly – eight in the first six months of 1996 alone – but confirmed ones are non-existent. Most of the 'photos' are easily unmasked as the wake of a passing boat or logs, floating vegetation, swimming deer, splashes of birds or elaborate hoaxes – one was even a picture of a dead horse floating down the loch.

Minor details like accuracy and existence have not

been allowed to get in the way of the legend of the Loch Ness Monster. Support for the theory has been drawn from sources as far apart as ancient Christianity and modern seismology. St Columba, who brought Christianity to Scotland, was the first monster-spotter. In AD565, it is said, he came upon a huge beast poised to attack a swimmer at St Ninian's, near Inverness. He banished it to Loch Ness. More than 1,400 years later, geologists and zoologists have devoted their careers to proving that the monster still lurks in the depths.

Apart from St Columba, however, the Church has remained at best sceptical. Not long after the phenomenon took off, a Fort Augustus minister wrote: 'The word "monster" is really not applicable to the Loch Ness animal, but is truly applicable to those who deliberately sin against the light of law and revelation.' In other words, come search for the monster if you must – but never on a Sunday!

Certainly, if Scotland was to have its very own monster, Loch Ness would be the obvious home for it. Deeper in parts than the North Sea, the loch has plenty of freezing cold water – indeed, it only gets above a chilly 12°C for four months of the year. But, the scientists say, that would be enough to keep a monster happy. Surveys of the loch floor have established that it could support life; certainly, there are shoals of fish even in the deepest parts, plenty to satisfy a monster's appetite. Sonar tracking has also indicated the presence of single, large objects – probably shoals of fish, but possibly a monster.

Some say the 'monster' could simply be a huge Baltic sturgeon, which returns to the loch every year to spawn. Others are convinced there really is a monster. Many simply believe it a product of over-fertile imaginations. Judge for yourself – watch carefully for tell-tale ripples on the surface which could give you the final proof. In the meantime, examine the evidence collected at the Loch Ness Monster exhibition centres while you are here in Drumnadrochit.

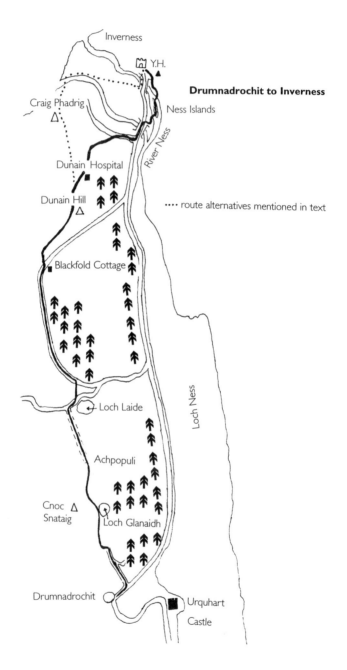

Inverness

Y.H.

Drumnadrochit to Inverness

Craig Phadrig

Ness Islands

River Ness

Dunain Hospital

Dunain Hill

···· route alternatives mentioned in text

Blackfold Cottage

Loch Laide

Loch Ness

Achpopuli

Cnoc
Snataig

Loch Glanaidh

Drumnadrochit

Urquhart

Castle

Section 8
Drumnadrochit to Inverness

The Great Glen Way is entering the home straight. This final section leads to Inverness, the bustling Highland capital. But it's not all over yet; ahead is the longest climb and the highest point on the Way: a fitting finale to the walk.

Inverness is the largest town in the Highlands but to reach it the Great Glen Way takes in the wildest terrain you will encounter on the walk, and makes greatest use of your navigational skills. It starts with a steep though fairly short climb out of Drumnadrochit before quickly heading into open moorland where paths are faint and, for a brief stretch, non-existent. You will have to take care not to stray from the route – the high moorland you will be walking through is vast and featureless so it is important to follow directions. In mist and fog, navigational skills will be particularly important. Even in the driest, sunniest weather, you may encounter areas of marsh and bog on the highest section, so good footwear is essential.

The route is, however, well within the capabilities of Way walkers. The two steep climbs on the last section were perfect training for the exertions to come, and you can always console yourself with the knowledge that once the initial ascent is over, it's downhill all the way to Inverness.

This is also the most varied section of the route. Leaving behind the bustle of Drumnadrochit and its monster-seekers, the route quickly enters farming country. Then follows the glorious, if more exposed, high moorland section, where bracken and heather blaze with colour on even the gloomiest of days. Then it is back to agriculture, interspersed with forestry plantations and expansive moorland until the urban sprawl of Inverness is reached. Do not be surprised if you find Inverness's crowds rather daunting – they will be a sharp contrast to the calm and tranquillity of the tracks and lanes on the Way from Fort William.

To begin this final section, head north on the A82 across the River Enrick then turn right to head along towards Loch Ness. Carry on along the road past the Bank of Scotland and the Official Loch Ness Monster Exhibition, one of the two devoted entirely to the elusive monster. After ten minutes of walking along the pavement, just after a small stone bridge across the Drumbuie Burn, turn left up a road heading to the settlement of the same name.

The road winds up the side of the burn, bordered by a profusion of trees and plants – snowdrops and daffodils in the early spring, bluebells, primroses and rhododendrons later in the spring and a variety of summer flowers. Head up past the modern buildings of Drumbuie Farm on the right (which offers bed and breakfast). The road climbs some way above the burn, its banks now covered mainly by silver birch trees. As you pause to catch your breath, enjoy the fine views back across Drumnadrochit and Loch Ness towards Castle Urquhart. The higher you climb, the more expansive the views get; eventually, you will be able to pick out the route of the Way as it descended from Bunloit, the domed summit of Meall Fuar-mhonaidh once again proving an excellent landmark. Make the most of the views of Loch Ness; they are the last on the Way.

A smattering of houses marks the end of the climb, and from here onwards the ground undulates far more gently. Some of these houses offer bed and breakfast – a handy overnight spot for those who think their last day's walk should be as unstrenuous as possible. As you pass Tigh Ruigh at the top of the hill, a road branches off right towards Achtuie Farm. The Way, however, turns left behind Tigh Ruigh, through a gate marked 'Torran' and across the Drumbuie Burn.

On the other side of the burn, the road curves to the left, heading westwards. The Way leaves it here and climbs up the bank a short way to the path which it will follow across the moor to Achpopuli. There is a path by the side of the burn, but the higher route offers a more

Looking back on the last day

direct – and usually drier – way across the moor, as well as giving better views over the surrounding countryside.

This gives you plenty of opportunity to appreciate the dramatic change in terrain. Gone are the trees and forest tracks, and no longer are there lochs to soften the scenery or canals to add a glint of silver. These are replaced by a large, undulating high plain, covered with heather and dotted with hawthorn and juniper bushes. You may spot the occasional pine tree, looking a little startled to have survived the attentions of sheep and deer long enough to have grown to a decent size. Scattered patches of alpine flowers grow here too – look for tormentil, saxifrage and alpine lady's mantle – a welcome patch of brightness in the muted browns, mossy greens and deep purples of the heather and bracken. You are now more than 250m (800ft) above sea level, almost at the summit of the Great Glen Way, and it will feel like it. Small hummocks rise around you and it is an easy stroll to the top of any of them to gain a view across the expanse of the moor.

Keep on the narrow path, which at times is little more than a sheep track, and stick to the high ground as far as possible. Small birds like tits, wagtails and dotterels jump up from the ground as you pass; occasionally a grouse, disgruntled at being disturbed, will lumber from the heath and laboriously take to the air; the cuckoo sings out its familiar call.

The path winds through the rolling hills to Loch Glanaidh, the source of the Drumbuie Burn, which nestles between peat hags about a third of the way along the moorland stretch of this section. Just before the lochan, the path widens out to a Land Rover track which continues along the side of the loch. Beyond the loch, the Way climbs above 350m (1,200ft), its highest point.

If you want to take a photo commemorating reaching the summit of the Way, it is marked by a cairn and a solitary small spruce. Just beyond here, the path peters out and you have to strike across country. Head between the two hillocks to the right in the north-east which lie on a line directly towards Achpopuli rather than descending towards the plantations ahead. Once through the gap between the hillocks, continue round the lower slopes of Meall na h-Eilrig, where you should pick up a faint path. When the farm buildings are in view, strike out across the moorlands towards Achpopuli Farm, taking care to shut gates and prevent damage to fences on the way.

The way continues through the farm and down a long, straight track flanked on either side by plantations of spruce trees. The easy walking of the track will be a relief after the spell of bog-trotting, particularly if the day is wet. The track ends at a small tarmac road where you turn right towards Loch Laide, which is renowned for its very pure water. Even if you do not want to risk a sip to test the truth of this claim, you may want to walk along to its shore to see the crannog, built in a similar way to Cherry Island on Loch Ness. The Way turns off the road before reaching Loch Laide, however, turning left after only 100m (325ft) on the road along the side of a plantation of larch trees. A clear but little-used track cuts along the side of the trees, continuing through a clear-felled section and a small copse of mixed trees until it meets the road from Abriachan which continues to Ladycairn.

If the felling has made the path hard to follow or if there is work in progress while you are on the route, take a detour instead through the small hamlet of Abriachan. Now just a small settlement, it was at one time a thriving crofting community. The local school once had a hundred children on its roll; by the time it closed in 1958, that figure had dwindled to just 12. By all accounts, it was a rather unruly community, too. The *Third Statistical Account of Scotland* records: 'The people of Abriachan were regarded by neighbouring districts as rough, uncultured and quarrelsome. They engaged in a lot of illicit whisky-making, using fires of heather and juniper which made little smoke.'

A little way down the hill beyond Abriachan is the old Killianan Church, dedicated to St Adamnan, abbot of St Columba. More interesting to would-be brides and grooms is the stone with a bowl-shaped hollow in it which lies in the thicket above the church. Couples who made their vows there were allowed a year's trial marriage, which could be dissolved if they did not get on, provided there had been no children.

To make the detour to Abriachan, continue on the road past Loch Laide until it joins the road which has climbed up from Loch Ness. Turn left at this fork and continue down through the forest towards Ladycairn.

The official Way joins the road from Abriachan just after it enters the forest. Turn left down the road and walk through the trees on the slow downhill march towards Inverness. Occasional clearings in the trees on the left give glimpses of the surrounding countryside, dotted with small crofts and steadings, and to the imposing hills beyond. To the right is Rinuden, site of a Bronze Age settlement and field system, which lies about a third of the way through the forest. At the end of the forestry plantation, the settlement known as Ladycairn marks a return to more agricultural territory. On the right just as you leave the forest are a few examples of ancient Scots pine.

As the road winds down towards Blackfold, the Great Glen comes into view once again, the steep drop from the green hills on the south-eastern side hinting at the unseen River Ness below. Beyond the edges of the Glen, hills stretch off into the distance. Far ahead, you will see the buildings of Blackfold, which mark the spot where the Way disappears into woods for the last time on its final descent into Inverness. The high peat hags at the edge of the road reveal traces of tree roots, indicating that this terrain was once far less empty and bleak than it seems now.

Scots pine is the only native British conifer – although it is now much less common than the ubiquitous spruce, fir and larch trees which make up much of the country's commercial forestry. The Caledonian pine forest, of which you have seen a few odd fragments as the Way has progressed through the Great Glen, once covered much of the north of Scotland. Although called pine, the ancient forest was in fact a wide mixture of trees. Birch trees came first, some 8,000 years ago, followed by hazel, oak and elm. Scots pine and alder did not appear until about 2,000 years ago.

The Caledonian forest may have taken more than 6,000 years to reach the height of its diversity, but it took less than 200 years for man to destroy it. All over Scotland, huge tracts were chopped or burnt down to make way for crofting, to deprive outlaws of places to hide and to smoke the much-feared wolf out of its hiding place. But it was the Highland clearances and the invasion of gentrified landowners wanting to use the land for sheep-farming and deer-hunting which sounded the final death knell. These voracious animals swallowed the young shoots as soon as they appeared, so the forests were unable to regenerate.

179

There is a growing recognition of the attraction of these original mixed forests, not just aesthetically but also in encouraging a variety of plants and wildlife and in protecting the soil from erosion. Most commercial plantations now have at least a screen of mixed wood to lighten the dull expanse of conifers, while in a number of areas – most notably at the National Trust-owned Mar Lodge near Braemar and Glen Coe – there are attempts to re-establish the ancient forest, initially behind a high fence to keep out the hungry deer.

The Great Glen had its own contributors to the destruction of the forest. Apart from the barrels and shipbuilding in Inverness mentioned earlier, Lochaber timber was used in the building of Holyrood Palace in Edinburgh in the 15th century, and oaks from Loch Ness were used to construct the cathedral in Fortrose 200 years later. The original fort at Inverlochy was built with timber in 1650, flouting a 200-year-old law intended to protect the forests. After the Jacobite rebellion, much of the forfeited land, including large tracts of the Great Glen, were bought up by the York Building Company. It set up iron smelters, including the one in Invergarry Castle, using charcoal produced from burning local trees for fuel.

The original Caledonian forest may have all but disappeared, but the replacements are the most important industry of the Great Glen. And, while we may occasionally resent the uniformity of the coniferous forests, we should be grateful that the Forestry Commission is willing to provide access. Without that welcome, walking the Great Glen Way would be impossible.

Blackfold cottage is the third house reached along the roadway, easily indentifiable by the wishing well and pergola in its garden. Opposite the house, a path strikes off to the left into the trees. Follow that, taking the right-hand fork when it splits after 100m, and head into the forest once more.

This section of the Craig Leach forest is an exception to the modern rule that plantations should be mixed. It is almost uniformly spruce, but the path is wide and the planting thin enough to give attractive variations of light and shade. When the path ends in a junction, take the left fork and continue on this track until it leaves the forest. A number of other tracks branch off it to the left and right, but you should ignore them all and stick to the main path. Eventually, it passes through a firebreak from where you get the first glimpses of the northern side of the Beauly Firth on the left. Its blue waters glint occasionally through the trees as you continue along the route, which climbs a little as it curls around Craig Leach Hill before dropping down again to pass under a row of pylons.

At the next fork in the track after the pylons, go left and continue along the side of Dunain Hill, where the mixed rowan, birch and other deciduous trees make a welcome break from the unrelenting spruce of the earlier part of the forest. Go over the stile next to the green gate and turn right along the road. Further along the main track from here lies the Leachkin chambered cairn, which is being cleared to allow visits. Beyond it is Craig Phadrig, the most famous of the Great Glen's vitrified forts. An alternative route into Inverness, which ends most fittingly at the eastern terminus of the Caledonian Canal, takes you past both these monuments. It is described at the end of the chapter.

Those heading into the centre of Inverness on the official Great Glen Way should turn right at another line

The forest above Craig Dunain

of pylons that crosses the track and head along a path that cuts between two lochs – the one on the left large enough to sport an island in the middle. A gate marks the end of the forest track from where you get the first glimpse of your destination. Inverness is spread out ahead, its buildings sprawled along the shores of the

Beauly Firth and the North Sea. If you look closely, you will be able to pick out the tell-tale red brick of Inverness Castle, the end of the Great Glen Way. It is still a good hour's walk away.

Go through the gate then walk diagonally across the field and out through another gate at the bottom. That brings you out onto a green road which curls down past a small golf course to the Victorian buildings of the Craig Dunain hospital. Opened in 1864, it was at the time a pioneering place for the treatment of the mentally ill. Previous 'treatments' had included being imprisoned in the thieves' pit in the old stone bridge, being dragged behind a ten-oar boat 'with all the speed that could be achieved', or burying a black olive at the place where someone had had an epileptic seizure. The hospital was something of a tourist attraction after its opening; the local paper records that 'a number of unmannerly and idle persons . . . have annoyed patients by going close to the windows and staring at them'.

The Great Glen Way continues on the road through the grounds of the hospital, which is shortly due to close. Once in the grounds, turn left towards the tall red chimney. At the main road into the hospital, go left again out of the hospital gates then turn right down the road immediately beyond the gates and continue for a few metres to a tall red gate. Go through this high kissing gate, which can be difficult to negotiate with a rucksack, and follow the path down between the fields to the outskirts of Kinmylies. Skirt round the back of the houses then turn right onto the grassed area between two of the houses which leads to a road through the estate. Cross the road and continue down a wide grassy path and behind the houses up to a busy road which serves the hospital and housing estates. Turn right along the road, passing through the centre of a golf course, until you reach the A82. From there, turn left and it is a short walk to the Caledonian Canal, seen for the final time on the Great Glen Way as it flows under the Tomnahurich bridge.

The bridge is named after the hill which rises above it on the east side of the canal, the bottom part of which is now a cemetery. The *Statistical Account* of 1799 described it as 'a beautiful, isolated mount, nearly resembling a ship with the keel uppermost'. That vision may have been inspired by the prophecy of the Brahan Seer, the Highland prophet Kenneth Odhar Mackenzie Lewis, who in the 17th century predicted that 'Strange as it may seem to you this day, the time will come, and it is not far off, when full-rigged ships will be seen sailing eastward and westward by the back of Tomnahurich at Inverness'.

Kenneth worked on the Brahan estate of the Earl of Seaforth and used a pierced blue stone to tell fortunes. Thomas Telford's canal-building may have proved his ship prophecy right, albeit 200 years later, but one of his other visions was to cost him his life. When the Earl of Seaforth was in Paris, his wife asked the Brahan Seer to find out his whereabouts. He replied that he could see the Earl kneeling before a lady and kissing her hand. So incensed was Lady Seaforth with this news that she ordered Kenneth to be executed by being plunged into boiling tar.

A little further back along the canal, at Torvean, canal workmen excavating the route of the canal in 1809 found a Pictish chain of solid silver, weighing seven pounds. A sign of rank worn on ceremonial occasions, it is now in the museum at Inverness.

Having crossed the bridge, turn right to walk down

the road at the side of the canal towards the River Ness and the last stage of your journey. Turn left as you reach the river then cross the small bridge which takes you onto the delightful Ness islands, with their attractive trees and shrubs. Cross another bridge onto the east bank of the river, then stroll along the bank until you reach Inverness Castle. Climb up the steps to the esplanade where a statue of Flora MacDonald waits to welcome you.

Having begun the Great Glen Way smelling the salt of the Atlantic by the walls of the old fort in Fort William, you finish it at the castle in Inverness – a fine end to a whirlwind tour through Scotland's turbulent history.

Alternative Route into Inverness

This route gives good views over the Beauly Firth and ends at the eastern sea lock of the Caledonian Canal. Instead of turning right at the pylons, carry straight on along the track underneath the pylons and down the hill. At certain times of the year – early summer is particularly fruitful – the path will seem like a toads' playground, the small black-marked reptiles leaping from the ground as you approach. The path descends gradually, flanked by a profusion of thistles, which come alive in summer with the flutter of butterflies.

The path joins a metalled road then continues downhill, the dark shape of Ord Hill looming across the Moray Firth ahead. At the first house on the left, take some time to savour the views across Inverness on the right. Passing the turning to Blackpark, the road descends more steeply, while ahead the red sandstone of Inverness Castle stands high above the town.

The road passes a Forest Enterprise carpark and walking trail on the left. Go into the carpark and take the yellow walking route for 80m (260ft) until it meets another forest track on the right. Take that track, on the blue forest walk, and continue uphill for a further 80m. Leave the forest walk on a narrow path which climbs steeply to the fort.

Craig Phadrig lies on top of the steep hill, a position which was clearly attractive to the Iron Age fort-builders for the open views all around – a perfect spot for a defensive building. Its most famous occupant was Bridei, son of Maelchon, king of the Picts from AD555 to 584. He had a palace near Inverness, which St Columba visited when he brought Christianity to the royal family in 565. An earlier fort on the site was defended by a

The descent from Craig Phadrig

186

stone wall interlaced with timber, which was set on fire about 400BC. Whether this was done by enemies or as part of the construction process is the subject of debate. The result was a fire which burned so fiercely that the stones melted together and fused in places.

Descend from the fort down a steep and rocky path on the opposite side to your approach. From here, Muirtown Basin at the end of the canal comes into view, meaning that the end of the Great Glen Way is now in sight. The path broadens after the initial tricky section, and a bed of gravel makes the walking easier. When you meet a wider track, turn right and continue until the track ends at a gate and stile. Climb over to the single-track road beyond and then turn right. Some 150m along the road you will pass some houses. A steep flight of steps leads down between two of the houses on the left. Go down the steps, cross the road at the bottom and take the little path which leads out of the small cul-de-sac on the left. It climbs down to the road below, from where you can cross the railway line to the canal.

It is worth climbing up to the Clanchattan Monument which lies at the top of the path to admire the view of the basin below. The path ends at a road bridge on the A862. Turn left to cross the bridge then go immediately right into Low Street. Walk up Low Street as far as the railway footbridge then turn left and pass between the houses and onto the towpath for the final time.

The Great Glen Way is not truly completed until you walk right along to the Clachnaharry sea lock which marks the eastern end of the Caledonian Canal. The administrative offices for the canal are at Clachnaharry while the workshops which serve the whole canal are at

Muirtown Basin, which lies just above the sea lock. Just by the canal office is a plaque commemorating Telford's achievements. It is a verse from a poem by Robert Southey, the poet laureate:

Telford it was by whose presiding mind
The whole great work was planned and perfected
Telford who o'er the vale of Cambrian Dee
Aloft in air at giddy height upborne
Carried his navigable road; and hung
High o'er Menai's Strait the bending bridge.

Opposite lies Muirtown Basin, built big enough – at 800 yards long and 140 yards across (732m by 128m) – to serve as a second harbour for Inverness. Ships soon grew too big for it, however, and it has never been well used.

The sea lock at Clachnaharry

Climb up to the road and turn left to walk into Inverness and the official end of the Great Glen Way at the castle. Castle Street was previously known as Doom Street because it was the route taken by condemned men on their way to the gallows near Ardkeen Tower.

Inverness Castle was the site of an early royal castle and, by 1718, it boasted a substantial tower house, two of whose bastions were added by General Wade. Now it consists of two buildings linked by a bastioned wall. The court-house at the southern end was added in 1843. The second building was originally a prison but later became county council offices before being turned into the town's second sheriff court.

It was not the only castle in Inverness, nor even its most famous. Macbeth's Castle, immortalised in the Shakespeare play as the scene of Duncan's murder, stood on a promontory in what is now the Millburn district of Inverness. Little of the play is based on reality – Duncan, for one, died in battle near Elgin. But Inverness did see its fair share of events which shaped Scottish history. In 1411, for example, it was sacked by the Lord of the Isles and, 17 years later, James I held a parliament there to express his displeasure at the constant warring of the northern tribes. To emphasise his point, he hanged some of the chiefs and imprisoned a number of others, including Alexander, son of the Lord of the Isles. Immediately he was released, he repeated his father's actions and burnt the town again.

Not everyone has been enthusiastic about the Inverness people. One of Telford's assistants remarked: 'With the possible exception of the Provost, there is none that wouldn't be better hung.' Nowadays, though, it is a welcoming, busy town, as befits the capital of the Highlands. There are numerous hotels, hostels and bed and breakfasts as well as a youth hostel and campsites. And there are plenty of pubs and restaurants where you can celebrate your achievement in completing the Great Glen Way.